THE
ADASTRA READER

THE
ADASTRA READER

BEING THE COLLECTED CHAPBOOKS
IN FACSIMILE WITH BIBLIOGRAPHY
AUTHOR NOTES & COMMENTS
ON HAND BOOK
MAKING

GARY METRAS

ADASTRA PRESS   Easthampton, MA

811.08
Ad 1
c. 2

ADASTRA PRESS
101 Strong Street
Easthampton, MA 01027

In the early days of printing the craftsman lavished his thought, and care, and skill on the presentation of a bit of worthy literature which we may cherish and enjoy today; his art was applied to things worth while. Today, the printer is asked to devote time, care, and money to producing works of ephemeral value, to publicity, or advertising, only a very small part of which, no matter how well it is done, escapes the wastebasket. Thus is wasted much of the time and thought and money that by rights should be applied to something more deserving of preservation.

--Frederic W. Goudy,
Typologia

Contents

Introduction

THE ADASTRA READER just might be the first
anthology of its kind in the country. Not simply
a bibliography listing titles and dates, type faces
and book dimensions as have been published about
many fine presses over the years, though this volume
does include such information; not merely a selection
of the "best" of Adastra Press as many literary
journals compile to celebrate some anniversary or
other, though this volume, in a manner of speaking,
includes this but in an expanded format. THE ADAS-
TRA READER reprints, in facsimile, every chapbook
from its letterpress founding in 1979 through 1986,
a total of twelve books by eleven poets. This version
of an anthology presents the complete line of a
publisher in one of its formats of publishing: the
chapbook, short, single author collections of poetry.
This anthology is, then, a unique portrait of one
small press viewed through the poetry chapbooks
it has published. ¶ However one may argue for
or against chapbooks and an appropriate definition
of them, one thing is clear about publishing poetry
in America today: the chapbook is popular. It may,
indeed, be the mainstay of poetry publication; it
certainly is for that segment referred to as small
press. For Adastra Press the chapbook is its especial
love. They give a healthy view of a poet's work.
They are relatively quick, easy and inexpensive
to produce, and they are ideal for utlizing antique
methods of manufacturing, i.e., handcrafted letter-
press editions which, hopefully, carry on the tradition
of printing going all the way back to the invention
of movable type in the fifteenth century. ¶ The
traits of an Adastra Press chapbook are heavy,
textured paper stocks, hand set type, hand sewn
signatures with square spine covers and a sense
of typography. In other words an Adastra chapbook
is a made thing, not a generated commodity. This
anthology, unfortunately, only allows the reader

to see and judge the typographic design of the chapbooks and not the other, equally important elements of fine printing. With the exception of this anthology's cover, all interior pages were printed by photo-offset on high speed, automatic presses, which is the usual printing technology at use in most of the industrial world. The cover, though, was printed by hand from hand set type, in the usual, if antiquated, technology of Adastra Press. It is my hope, in combining the two technologies of printing, to widen the audience for the poets I've published beyond their limited editions and to educate the reader to the fact that fine book making, even if on a very limited scale, continues in our culture. This is not to say, of course, that Adastra Press is the only one currently keeping the old book arts alive. Far from it. Many individuals and groups are doing exactly this, to their and all of our credit.

II

Adastra Press is a one man operation. I do as much of the work as my equipment and stamina allows. My equipment and methods are antique: hand set type, hand fed platen letterpress. The paper is hand folded and sewn by hand and hand glued into a cover. I do the work as a hobby with my only reward being the joy of antique printing combined and enriched by the joy of the poets I've published when they express their wonder at what I've made out of their manuscripts. When other rewards such as a good review or an order from some stranger comes along, they are secondary, though somewhat important to the economic survival of Adastra. ¶ It is my desire that a well made book not be out of the financial reach of anyone; therefore the books and chapbooks I publish are not outlandishly priced, ranging from $2.50 to $15.00, which is, sadly, not the norm for publishers who are also fine printers and who mostly cater to collectors, whether individuals or institutions, whose main interest in the books they purchase is not the literature, itself, not the book, itself, but the hope for profitable return on their investment. Such collectors and publishers do literature no service and the writers even less as it is the book dealers who usually make the money, not the writers. ¶ Adastra Press publishes mainly little or unknown poets. It is they who are frequently excluded from fine publication because of the ecomonics of collecting. Besides, it's more fun working with such poets. They are usually more appreciative; they know, can see, can irrefutably hold in their hands the fact that someone else sweated over their poetry and did so for the love of the art--written or graphic. And if the poets are already known and have published collections previously, their reputations are probably small enough, given the nature of the literary, especially poetry readership in our culture. ¶ Being a small press publisher, in whatever format, is like being a poet. One works at some regular job and then in the off-hours writes, prints or publishes, and in some cases does all three. For the vast majority of writers and publishers in this country, literature is a hobby. A donation of labor and love. Some donate more. And some love more. But the end result is literature, whether good or bad. If the intentions are good, the results are never wholly bad. Writing poetry, publishing poetry is an extension of self, a reaching out to other selves; a community; almost a family. This is what small press and poetry are. And like a family or community, there are differences and disagreements between and among its members. Fair enough. There is room for all.

III*

Often I get such responses as "The book is beautiful," "a work of art," "just holding it in my hands, turning its pages, gives me such pleasure," to the books I've printed. At first these statements, however welcomed, were bothersome. But considering the glut of mass market paperbacks where the only attention to design is the cover and whose pages fall out when read and turned, I began to see why readers reacted this way to hand set type, handsewn signatures of hand fed letterpress books printed on heavy, textured papers. I even went so far as to theorize that good, faithful readers of books have some sort of deep-seated need to be elated with a book's printing, its design and paper, that, indeed, there may even be something sexual in the fondling of a well-made book. ¶ If this was really going on in the head of readers of such books, then I would continue for them--for their frustration with mass market production based on profit more than anything else, for their frustration with many small press publishers who manage to produce some excellent literature on meager budgets but which primarily satisfy the intellect and not the sensual needs of those good and willing readers. We do, after all, live in an age dominated by sensuality, whether in fine dining, designer jeans, hang gliding, walking in woods, white water canoeing, doing drugs or climbing mountains. All motivated by satisfying sensual urge. To make us feel. And this feeling gives us our lives themselves--defines our lives for us. For these appreciative hedonists, I make

---

*This portion of the Introduction is reprinted from Oro Madre magazine, where it first appeared under the title "Printing the Old Way."

the books I do. ¶ Besides, when I seclude myself in my cool, damp cellar on those stifling New England August afternoons and nights and take the soothingly cool steel and lead of composing stick, type and press in my hands, or spend the winter evenings and weekends in the cellar air almost as cold as outside, with the space heater trying to dissipate the mist of my breath, and hold that steel and lead colder than the snow piled against the foundation a few feet from my head, I am moved in my body and being as not even a wife can move me. I stand or sit at the bank of type cases smelling the old, warped wooden drawers and stands, the faint odor of ink and cleaning fluids, and always the old dust in the crevices, dust that might be fifty years old for I'd never fully cleaned the old things I bought, and the dust would twitch my nose. And I'd smile. A warmth deep inside spreading outward. ¶ Feverishly I place each individual metal letter in its place, one letter at a time, one line of a poem at a time until a page is set. At those times the world ceases to exist. There is only this plodding task at hand. This joy in small, old things. But every now and then I pause. Look the few feet down the row of type cases. And swear that, briefly, ever so briefly, the figure of Gutenberg, of Jenson or Caxton appear, their hands with fat wrinkled fingers hurriedly dipping into the crowded slots of type drawers to retrieve a letter and place it in the stick held in the other hand to complete a line. And once or twice, he, whichever one it was that time, hunched over the type, his leather apron well stained and dangling below the knees, he would turn to face me, sternly nod and vanish. ¶ Of course it's a fantasy. A delusion of self-importance. A phony maintaining of a long out-moded tradition which, for all practicality, is worthless by today's standards of computer-photo type composition which can set up to 120 lines per minute where I manage only two; of foot-pumping a printing press and hand feeding single sheets of paper where the high-speed web offset presses of today turn out 15,000 plus pages of five colors an hour on continuous feed rolls of paper and automatically cut, collate, gather and staple. But some of my type was cast around WWI. And my press was made in 1882. The current generation

CLOSE-UP SHOWING LEADS BETWEEN LINES OF TYPE

of computer printing equipment will be outdated in five years or less. Hundreds of thousands of dollars spent on equipment to print <u>Time</u> magazine and Harlequin Romances that are thrown away on machines that will be thrown away. ¶ When Warren Campbell, type and book designer, says in <u>A Short History of the Printed Word</u>, "When the purpose of printing is to produce cheap, disposable copies, as is the case with paperbacks, high-speed rotary presses are functional and acceptable. Such means, however, seldom provide the esthetic aspect of reading--the feel and look of a good page that is just as desirable in the twentieth century as it

was in the fifteenth" he has been in that special world of fondling well made books and antique printing equipment and methods. He, too, has probably felt the presence of ghosts. When the poets whose books I've printed tell me they receive more comments from friends and readers on the type, paper and binding than on their poetry, I can only smile. Whether their poems will last, I don't know. I've clothed them in a lasting form. Whether the books themselves will last, I don't know. But in someone's cellar, the tradition of making a book a work of art through the old ways will survive if we survive.

IV

To return to this anthology: The twelve chapbooks which follow are arranged in order of appearance. They are fairly rendered from their original editions, which means that each is relatively complete. There are some omissions. Title pages have not been reproduced (with the exception of MENTIONING DREAMS) in favor of the covers which are usually more interesting in design. Nor have copyright, content and colophon pages, when they exist in the originals, been included here. There are separate appendixes at the end of this volume which replace these pages and render them redundant. Besides, their inclusion would have been a distrac-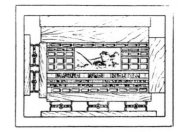tion to the entity which is this READER. The pagination of the original editions has been dropped to number the pages of this anthology as a consecutive whole. With several of the individual chapbooks, foot of the page decorations were used along with page numbers. These decorations have been reproduced where I felt their absence would hurt the page design and balance of the various individual chapbooks. This might create an odd reading effect as far as continuity of the entire anthology is concerned, but remember, each of these chapbooks, which I am now tempted to call chapters in this lengthy volume, was first designed and published as an individual work, and some of their flair should stand, especially in a collection such as this. ¶ Part of the personal joy in assembling this volume has been reviewing my work as an editor and printer. I hope that the reader will be able to judge for himself whether I have improved in either or both. I have so far been able to refrain from saying much about the poets and the poetry included here. As for the poets, each has supplied material for his and her own biographic note, appended to this volume. The poetry stands for itself as it should and does not require comments from me as publisher. The astute reader, in addition, will be able, should he desire, to form his own ideas about the kind of poetry I lean toward without, again, my having to meddle in the reader's judgments by interjecting personal esthetic tastes. Remember: freedom of the press belongs to whoever owns the press. ¶ Lastly, I dedicate this book to my own family, who have had to bear with my absences, even if I only disappeared to the cellar, with the books and papers piled throughout the house, with the mails and delivery trucks, the telephone calls, the strangers coming and going into their lives; and also to the poets who have allowed me to clothe their words with what skills I have: I love you all.

Gary Metras
Easthampton, Massachusetts
August 1986

THE CHAPBOOKS

THE NECESSITIES

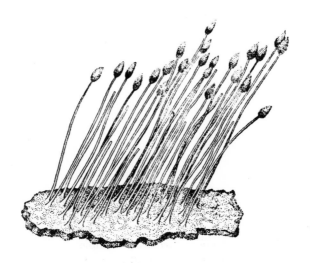

GARY METRAS

for Jason

See, now it calls us together
to bear parts as the whole.
Helping you will be hard.
—Rilke

1   DESTINATIONS

They say it will soon snow

Two things
will be renderred   How
we came to be here
and the direction of departure

As easy as that

as if tangents are irrelevant
just another clue to add to the list
of disorders

The white expanses will not stay white
Again wind affects the scene
Old habits will return
dressed for hard weather

The Russians believed a man was
defined by the boots he wore
and not the ones
packed in boxes

like desires

2 SKY

It is a condition only
of this world
an accident   some say
that broke the fall of sun's light
and left this blue
to worship

The probability of it happening
elsewhere

But there are other things
to calculate

The meaning of a kite when
the string snaps
What position to assume
to behold heaven
How far is the flight
of will alone

On a mountaintop there are
two choices
and one chance to descend

Even if it takes something
a million years to fall
fall it must

3 FORTUNES

I stare into
the face of a gypsy as she
reads my palm

Her line of eyebrow
and nose
train on my hand

like a gunner's sight
Yet those dark fingers   slender
soft as the tent's earth floor

so sure of themselves
like her hair
blacker than night

There will be one love
You will meet her again and again
Only one child will live

It is ancient business
these tellings of unknowns
and little speaks for it

except these returnings
in the hope
she'll get it right yet

4   A GAME

For now there is nothing
You and I sit by the window
and wait for the thing

that changes us

One bird is a myth
The blue falls heavy with questions
Wind has its affects
Shadows spoor under the evergreens

We are all eyes
feeding on dreams
and getting fat in the stillness

There are no rules
for this
except the ones that make us

5 CONTENTS OF POCKETS

Again that dream

The desk sergeant orders me
to empty my pockets on the counter

I have nothing I tell him

You lie he shouts

then shrugs when he sees my linings
and seals the envelope empty
puts my name on it
makes me sign for it

That's the procedure he says

Anyway   it's an old game
this search for motive

And I grow numb to the clues

And sleep has designs of its own

6 SHADE UNDER SPRUCE

Someone drives by thinking he's alone

For him the scenes passed will repeat
House   lawn   shrub
The palette of leaves
A silo in its quiet struggle
Hill   field   forest

as predictable as the children
waving at roadedge
For them a passing thing is a breeze
a moment arresting play
or a quick new game

honking
or ignoring in speed
Either way arrival is assumed
like moths in night
or children at play

And the shade under spruce

thicker than sound
with motions still as a planet
and hues of otherness

follows each of us

7 TIME FOR A STORY

Clouds fell on mountains
as if desperate
Winds moved into the empty rooms
And the sun and the moon
were as ghosts

One among us had a vision

Leave a boy child on the mesa
a feather in each hand
For nine days retrace your steps
so the tears fall
where you have already been

All this was done

and the day following
a bird of wings large as man
flew over the valleys
And clouds fled before him
And he shone golden in the sun

Know that he is Eagle
and when he soars
secure is the roof of the world

Such are the words
of the seer of things

and the deeds of the believers
who gave the story to sons
and they to theirs

as I to you
though understanding
is beyond us

8 DIRECTION OF WIND

For some time now
I have promised myself
to map the winds around this place
and see if there
are patterns
I don't know of

but the wind shifts so often
accuracy
is impossible

Trees lean one way
then another
Leaves gather where winds cross
are impotent

When I stand in the wind
it scatters me
and I fight the urge
to strip naked
and go where wind goes

9 FLOOD

The warnings always went ignored

War   earthquake   famine

Who could believe such frenzies

Pestilence   drought   disease

Then it rained so long traveling
became hazardous
even on the old   familiar ways

Things got loose
Trees   houses   governments
freed from the law of straight lines

Even the dead wouldn't stay put
floating past in those boxes
as if they were waiting for this

and just this

Ice   fire   flood

10 SONG

It repeats
like the call of an owl
the one song in the blank spaces
at the edge of wind
that won't leave you alone

Each time it sounds
you toy with small notes
picking each up
to hum in what light there is
to see if this is the one
to fly with through darkness
only to set them down
in their right place or not
more anxious than ever

Bits of old tunes stir in the pines
like a refuge dreamt of for years
where all the shadows are familiar
circling about on mice feet
A mossy voice comes
like an arm slipping around the body
These melodies could last years
if not for the scars of talons

What else is there to do
but pace in all the worn spots
The house sleeps
windows gone empty
The old habits return easy enough
Again weather is the excuse
the clouds not right fot singing
or there is no moon
just the waiting

The call repeats
swooping through night
full of its own necessity
until everything else goes unanswered
and the shunned distances merge
their edges drifting in
to where you sit
beginning to sing the one song
that has been there
all this time

poems by

ANDY GUNDERSON

For mother and in memory of father

While Asters
On the Hill
Their Everlasting fashions set
And covenant Gentions frill!

—Emily Dickinson

NIGHT·SHIFT

September has come
And I sit alone
With the quiet of plants
As they nod in soft light
Beneath the grey sky.

Tonight I will
Dress in the clatter
Of dishes at the EMproium
As my body
Rushes about tables
Beneath the dim lights.
The evening faces
Full of demands,
And the soft embraces
Of my waiter's voice
Become the night's rhythm.

In the morning
A soft fire will burn
Into the quiet of the afternoon
And the silent desires.

AUTUMN BIRDS

The autumn birds
Fill the dying elm.
A mote circles,
Dives and recircles.
The years slip through
Fingers like drunken
Nights. How many times
Will birds noisily
Gather, their black
Forms blown on the wind
Like an endless stream
Of dark leaves
Flying up.

THE ALLEY DOGS INCREASE

The alley dogs have returned
To the Haberdashery. At first
There was only one boney, black
Ghost of a dog meekly licking
A plastic garbage bag. I thought
He would never live through
The winter, but now he
Returns with others.
I have seen them since
Running through the empty
Lots in the Indian section
Or begging on the West Bank.
Last week the Mexican
Janitor and I laughingly tossed them
Restaurant scraps. Today I ask
In the little Spanish
I know, "Como estas los tres
Perres?" He laughs and says,
"Quatro. Quatro."

THERE IS
A POEM

There is a poem danced
By the graceful, dark limbs
Of the trees outside the window.

All winter I have glanced at them.
Like the black-stockinged
Legs of beautiful women, they
Have haunted my thoughts.

Last night they were trimmed with
White lace, but tonight has left
Them black, twisted and posing,
Black on black.

I wonder about
My inability to write a poem
Worth their attention.

WINTER REMORSE

Go away spring!
Let me keep in winter's room
  A cool mote—
One more stilled tendency.

THE SEA-GREY CLOUDS

The sea-grey clouds, the blue
White and chilly grey
Reflect in trapped water
Of a nearby roof.
The telephone wires
Streak and ripple
Across the surface.
The stark poles, their barren
Stance, like huge frozen
Ants holding their
Black, dusty streamers,
Mock an alley of green trees.

BLOSSOMS FLOAT IN THE ELMS

A gentle breeze blows in
From the north. Yellow
Blossoms float in the elms.
Their black branches silhouette
The tempered golden brick
Museum trimmed in white marble.
Tomorrow the blossoms will
Turn a redish brown and
Drift away. But now the elms
Sway in the breeze and their
Dark branches are like slender
Girls who pose then
Dance in yellow gauze.

STILL LIFE

An African violet in
Full bloom
In a fish bowl
On a black walnut
Vanity (now a desk)
Where a black phone
Squats beside a worn black
Dictionary and the blurred
Ripple of keys next to
A book closed on its
Poems and the coffee
(Walnut in a Chinese cup)
gets darker.

The night birds cry
And I have only this
Circle of light
And a few soft words.

COSMOLOGICAL

Planets and a few asteroids
Quietly go about their business.
Other things are dark
And silent. A comet
Or two slips by, testing
Its horn, and is barely noticed.

Further still a world
Flashes red as if to
Shriek emergency.

But the silence is
Too thick and
Time floats in
Stellar sleep through
The empty nova
Of its own light

Above the not quite dead
Jet black parking lot.

CITY PAUSES

After a light rain
The alleys get their only cleaning.
The day-trapped moon
Slips behind the blocked horizon.
In the street below
A stooped figure seeks
Refuge from night.
Across the street, on Jo Henri's
windowsill, a cat
Carefully washes.
Every now and then
He pauses to stare
At the silent, bird-filled trees.

SUMMER EFFECT

Loring Park lives
With shadowed figures
Strolling silently, or cluttered
In mute groups, eyes
Timid and hungry.
On the far side
Of the man-dredged lake
One figure struggles
Along the shore
Under tossing elms.
Wind blows his coat
And tosses about in lamplight.
The way the lake curves,
The dark, dreaming figures
Make the park look like
The gardens of
The asylum of Saint-Remy.

ESCAPE BY NIGHT

White clouds tinged in azure
Rush beneath the navy sky
And the crystal tint of stars.

Bats circle, light fluttering
In their intense eyes.

Oak and elm twist the night.

A moth on beige wings
Is caught between the lights
Flitting across my face.

FROM AN AGE OF

CARS

poems by

MERRITT CLIFTON

Korner Koin-Op, San Jose

Toward one Tuesday morning
the poor folk wash;
speak in Spanish of food stamps,
diarhea, sex, and their troubles;
quarrel, tired and stupid.
The husband, a browbeaten 25
pushing 50, jokes to end it.
The wife, a two-ton twenty
with plump, smooth tits he worships,
quashes him cold; scolds the baby
for smiling
and dully contemplates her burdens.
The baby, sloping forehead furrowed,
bright eyes wide,
accepts this as life.
While his mommy reads **The Enquirer,**
he pounds his daddy's head with both fists.
He coos.
His daddy laughs.
His mommy scowls.
Toward one Tuesday morning.

Caveman Wrestling, Friday Night

They crouch beneath the neons—
'Tag Teams! Live Intercourse!
Incredible Action!'—
behind the ropes, snarling, gnashing teeth.
Shining foreheads, black & white,
slope toward jut-jaws; noses flat,
hair curled, dark, moist; arms, legs, and
chests well-muscled, hairy. Erections protrude
from fake fur loincloths
like cannon from casements.
Palms dangle near knees, loose but ready.
The crowd eats popcorn, sips soda, guzzles beer,
buys programs.
"Kill the honky!" bursts from the peanut gallery,
"Kill the nigger!" from ringside.

Behind the wrestlers, clinging to their rumps,
mock-cowering while hissing insults,
wait their women.
Each wears a teasing imitation
leopard or zebra toga,
revealing siliconed breasts, plump thighs,
red lipstick, black gloves, net stockings,
spike heels.
One black, the other white,
both peroxide blondes. Both about thirty.
Harsh lights expose scars.

The referee stands, dressed like Elvis,
rhinestones glittering.

"You know the rules, boys," he says. "No gouging,
biting, blows to back, groin, or kidneys.
Butt-fuck the other guy to put him out of action;
fuck his woman to win the purse.
Shake cocks and come out fighting."

On steroids and speed, they nod.
Auditorium packed. They split a buck
off each five-buck ticket.
Sure beats the docks. Or one-night stands.
Tensing, they await the bell.

7/9/79, Anno Domini

GRENADA, Spain:
Twelve hundred partially mumified
men, women, and children were discovered today
sitting, standing, or sprawled in a crypt
beneath the quake-twisted cathedral tower.
Bones broken, limbs wracked, eyesockets gouged—

But not by the Inquisition, priests assure us.
Here were merely stored the corpses
of Jews, Moslems, and heretics
who sought sanctuary with their benevolent order.
The injuries?
The Church always took a special interest
in cripples.

MANAGUA, Nicaragua:
About the ruined cathedral here,
Red Cross workers this morning found
nine young men, ages twelve to sixteen,
wrists bound, blindfolded,
machine-gunned. Smouldering charnel pits
contain charred bones of others.

They still call this the New World.

Verdict

Judge Solomon Hacker, they say,
hates nigras worse than any other man
in the state of Missouri.
Chopped one up bad with his chainsaw once.
Runs a logging and woodcutting gang.
Took in a partner once, one Stump Atkins,
whom nobody known an' nobody seen.
Died a while back.
Got a wife, but nobody knows her.
She don't come to town.

Judge Solomon Hacker got an eighth-grade
diploma. Holds court in the general store yet,
his black Bible the only lawbook.
Last lay jay-pee in the state.

Makes good money, they say. Stingy, though.
Still lives in a tarpaper shack his grandpap built,
up top Hacker's Hill. His dogs are mean as he is.
Chaw your arm or leg off for settin' foot near it.

They say Judge Solomon Hacker never joined the Klan
'cause he's just plain too ornery.

What nobody knows is, Judge Solomon Hacker
ain't never paid himself one red cent.
Hacker's half of the business

built the clapboard Baptist church
an' stocked the county library
with Darwin, Blake, an' Twain.
That slim, soft-spoken, coffee-skinned black lady
who runs the charity thrift store
is Stump Atkins' daughter, hitched to Hacker
twenty-four years, eleven months now.
Sneaks down the hill to do her work.
Got two kids went to college on football scholarships.
Atkins hisself was the nigra he chainsawed;
he'd raped a white woman.

"Justice has been done," the judge told the mob,
saw still in his hands, spitting blood.
"Someone tar the stub." He made them put out
their torches, and take their shotguns home.

'Course, he wasn't the judge then,
an' Atkins was a stranger, just passin' through.

That does get told sometimes.

What four men in town ain't never gon' tell
is how for vengeance they raped young Dorothea Atkins,
come to claim her father at the Catholic hospital.
Kept her hogtied for hours, till the judge
heard her wimper.

His chainsaw bit through the door of the pumphouse
where they did their dirty-work, in hoods and sheets.
"Get them devil's robes off or I cut 'em off!"
the judge ordered. He made them kiss her feet.
Took her home, her an' Stump both.

For their twenty-fifth anniversary,
and his retirement,
Judge Solomon Hacker's gonna remarry her,
this time right out in public.
Ain't nobody gonna speak a word against it,
he warns the mirror. Shoulda done it years ago,
but he didn't like to break the myth: since he became judge,
no black man's been charged with a felony
in all his district. And not very many of anyone else.

A hard man, Judge Solomon Hacker.

In Terminal Shock

I die for my country, the president claims.
Yet on this desert plateau
my bones shall make no grass grow greener.

I die for my God, the chaplain tells me.
Yet my flesh is but a buzzard's sacrament,
a maggot's host.

I die for those at home, the sergeant growls,
without conviction.
Would my girl have me dead? Would any girl?
My mother, sister, brother?
My father? —My God, why hast thou forsaken me?

I die for the living, a comrade urges.
My bowels convulse, last erection jetting sperm
into guts, rags, and sand, to scald unfruitful.

I die for my comrades, yearns an inner voice,
four of whom fell in their attempted rescue.
More may follow; Marines never
leave their dead behind,
though many leave their behinds dead.

I die for freedom, the hometown news will report
—in uniform I was forced to wear,
in fight I never picked,

in land I never chose to visit,
before I was allowed the legal beer
I long for.

I die for peace.
My own peace. My own death, unwilling,
beneath the shriek of shells
and high, indifferent sun, baking me back
into clay I came from.

Cambodia, 1/1/80

This silo choked with skulls
and that with bones;
and what I wonder is,
why stockpile death?

Ain't no shortage of that.

Pre-trial Examination

Chained to the chair, the madman smiles
as psychologists pace the room—
"So! You want to be Jesus!
Delusions of grandeur, eh?—you with a halo,
the whole world kneeling? Hah!
Rewards must be earned; you're no angel."

He responds in slow monotone—
"I seek no recognition."
And falls swiftly silent.

They pounce—
"Ah! Masochism, is it? Self-worth
through persecution and pain.
Sexual release
in beatings, thorns, nails?"

"I would endure them," he says,
"if necessary."

Pipes blow smoke, matches and tempers flaring.
"What, what, what then?"

He raises manacled hands.
"To free, with my touch, the innocent prisoners."

"That you might be thanked and exalted?"

"No," he grins, "more selfish still.
That the world I made
might at last be perfect."

Literate Graffiti

4/25/80—DAWN RAID

Clock-radio. 8 Marines dead.
Window, stretch.
Buzzards circle the eastern field.

MEWING IN THE BARN

The slinking black cat,
green eyes narrowed,
didn't drown her own kittens.

Derelicts

I. COMSAT

In sinking orbit about a long-dead planet,
last trace of living inhabitants,
it emitted but one steady signal:
"bleep-bleep. . . bleep-bleep. . .",
perhaps an improvised S.O.S., we speculated,
then a dirge,
now a kaddish.

But sifting among dusty white ruins,
whose walls broke like stale brown sugar,
probing mechanical artifacts burnt and melted
into hard, dry raisins,
we learned it was but a jammer,
protecting sweet eyes and ears
from tart entertainment.

II. ICBM

We thought the drifting hulk,
almost beyond their solar-system,
might prove a time-capsule,
bearing their tale, with whatever they could give.
It did, we knew, in the searing blast.

Opening the Barrow

Longship, weapons, rings & carvings,
&, a tribute to his valor,
a youug woman,
clubbed from behind
as she knelt.

Her warm & gentle hands
kneaded the bread
that ants find
soon after the diggers.

Artificial Squid, Cape Cod 5/14/80

for **LORNA DEE CERVANTES**

Picking shells, she finds it,
disc-like skeleton
trailing translucent,
perforated tentacles
in precise spiral curve.

A species adapted
to survive oil-slicks—
sun-dried & stiffened
among the blackened kelp
and bones of rays
and tarry feathers,
but still leaking black to the touch.

"Fits any V-8," I read,
taking it from her.
"Change every 2,000 miles."

Letter from an Iranian Seamstress

To the Outlaws, Hell's Angels, Satan's Disciples—

Dear Brothers In Struggle:

We hear by short-wave Radio America
how, when you ride your motorcycles,
you do not wear crash-helmets.
We hear how you ride in demonstration
to state capitols; how you risk fines,
imprisonment, even death
to feel the breeze and face the dangers
you choose.

It is the same with us.

Your government calls you evil men.
We cannot judge. Ours calls us evil women;
whores, because we do not wear chador and veil.
We too are fined, jailed, beaten,
sometimes even stoned, buried to the waist alive.

We are alone, without men who understand.

Brothers, will you ride for us?

From an Age of Cars

I never knew why men revere the horse,
why women would make love to centaurs,
until we opened the Ming tomb
where buried alive
lay a household, court, and harem
with all their animals.

Some suffocated or starved as stoics,
some in yellow terror.

But a deep, long gash
in solid stone
shows how the horse resisted.

Amid his bones
the hooves were gone—

I think of Pegasus,
of Apollo's steeds,
who flew to life
and did not need hooves.

MATTERS OF THE HEART

AND OTHER POEMS BY W. D. EHRHART

for Anne Senter Gulick

RHYTHM

The rhythm
comes through his hands.
That's what the old man told me.

Sits all day by the waterfront
catching fish.
Big fish.
Twelve inches long.

Pulls living creatures
from this stagnant
oil-encrusted
cesspool of a harbor
where the last fish
must have died
thirty years ago.

I asked him how he does it.

"It's the rhythm that gets 'em,"
he said;
"And the rhythm
comes through my hands."

AGAIN, REHOBOTH

I have stood by this bay before.
I have watched the light from the moon
dance in the eyes of friends
while the moon danced on black water;
wanting to know where you were,
exactly what you were thinking.

There was a time when I thought
a man could suffocate
in the dark abscess of want;
a time when I didn't believe
tomorrow would come
except in the shape I gave it.

You belong to that time—you
and the tears that fell in the wake
of the false peace of October
when it still seemed possible
to wield light like a sword.

I am a teacher now;
I live alone.
I am anchored to this world
by all cold necessity
holds sacred: water, salt,
the labored rhythms of breathing.

I cherish my friends,
whose thin threads spread like glowing wires
out from the center, bending away
over the four horizons
in smooth unbroken lines,
and the quiet slap of the water
kissing the land.

When did the recognition come—
the slow submission of dreams; the wind
turning to blow down the years
like a steady silence—
things seem hardly to have changed
at all: these hands; this head
with its wild brown mane;
this heart still beating.

Evening approaches; already
the first star burns in the east.
There will be no moon tonight.
Out on the bay, the boats beat home
to the seagulls' plaintive cries,
their smooth bending sails
blood-red from a fire sun.

NEAR-SIGHTED

Christy is eighteen.
She is learning to master
the knowledge of generations
to make dreams
a three-dimensional living future
of wood, and steel, and pure light on brilliant
white stone surfaces soft as human skin.
The dreams are hers—
they come in the night,
and keep her awake for hours;
in the morning she goes to class
sleepy, and eager. The energy
                    is awesome:
she is every child; she dreams all vibrant
possible dreams; some of them are mine.
She doesn't understand the hollow stalker
war—the skeleton, the bandit;
she doesn't see the scarred carcasses
of salmon floating in still pools
along the banks of gray foam-speckled rivers;
she doesn't hear the starving angry
voices shouting for bread. She believes
in tomorrow; I believe
                    she is important:
when the rage rises, I want to beat
my fists upon the blind

heads of governments, the money kings,
the scientists and soldiers: "why
are you stealing Christy's dreams? Are you all
without children of your own?"
                                        Sometimes,
I am unfit to live with.
It is hard to remember—
if we blow ourselves to hell,
or choke, or starve to death,
the pages of my books fluttering
in the wind pouring in between
the cracked bricks of Christy's buildings,
all the yellowed bones of obsolete humanity
strewn like old cars in fields beside roads,
the unborn generations permanently blind—
something will survive:
dolphins, perhaps; opossums;
the scuttling, clicking crabs;
those iron-plated roaches we forever crack
jokes about, as though our nervous laughter
could hold true progress
in check.

Something will survive—
if only a dark cold lump
whirling through the silence
between the stars; the stars,
the billions on billions
of stars.

THE TRAVELER

All winter long
I watched you prepare:
one by one
your leaves turning pale,
curling, brown at the edges;
each silent morning
another lying on the windowsill.

The others say you are dying.

I knew all along
you were only passing through.

When you reach the end,
tell the one who sent you
I gave you water.

THE DANCERS

The audience knows
only what it sees:
dancers
gliding over the floor to music,
the beat of a drum, silence—
turning arching melting whirling
starburst form: tears
where hands should be;
love in a graceful
parabolic curve:

Beads of sweat
dropping from the temples,
hearts knocking, pulses on fire
can't be seen—nor the hours,
nor the days, nor the months,
nor the fear, nor the knowledge
that it's never good enough,
never finished: every bone, every fiber,
every gesture of the dancers
     straining
in the unforgiving moment of performance
to achieve the illusion of ease.

The audience only knows
what it sees.

FOG

Snow all night; and then the temperature
up fifteen degrees before dawn:
white slush, wet sludge beneath,
not fit for anything—not even children;
and the fog curtaining up from the ground
luminous, so thick you have to part it
as you walk, and duck quickly
under branches out of nowhere.
You know today the sun is shining
somewhere, but it isn't here.

Here, the day is wrapped tightly
in a white shroud shivering thoughts
out of places no one ever visits
on an ordinary day, though admission price
is cheap (free), and never varies:
see yourself the way you really are—
the way, at least, light bent through fog
makes you seem when all reassurances
are gone, it's Sunday, you live alone,
and even the telephone won't ring. Funny

how the good seems nebulous as fog.
Wrong ways, wrong words, wrong decisions
hammer like a blacksmith on an anvil:
people you will never see again come back

real as people you will have to face tomorrow—
and if you've done it wrong, you've done it
wrong so many times it hurts to be alone
on days like this with thirty years of flaws
and nothing in the house but bourbon.

Well, it's good bourbon, and it's almost
evening now. Snow and mud are freezing;
fog is lifting; clear sky, perhaps,
by morning. So you go to sleep
listening to the silence broken
only by the hammer—waiting
for an ordinary day to set you straight.

THE ERUPTION
OF MOUNT ST. HELENS

(for Nimimosha of the Bear Tribe Medicine Society)

Ash fallout is the hot news here."
Too far away to feel or hear the blast,
Nimimosha watched the gray-brown cloud
rising and advancing east
until the land and all living things
lay blanketed in ash, and her daughter's
infant eyes burned red with grit;
then she went inside.

"If it rains lightly now," she writes,
"the ash will turn to caustic paste
and harden to dissolve slowly,
burning the earth as it goes.
We're concerned about the fish"—
jellied mud on surfaces of ponds
and lakes, blocking oxygen exchange;
"the cows are eating ash-coated grass,
drinking ash-coated water,
blinking ash-coated eyes.
Then there are the horses. . . .

"We must stay inside.
The highways all around Spokane

are blocked; telephones are down;
everything is closed. We're thankful

"things are not too bad: even though
the day turned black at noon, the world
continues, and we're all still here.
The feeling here is powerful.
Walk in balance on Mother Earth."

My ash-coated heart soars
to where she is—as if desire alone
could lift the burden of her hardship,
clean the water, feed the cows, wipe
the burning grit from Yarroe's eyes—
and yet I cannot cry:

Nature's fury lacks the malice
of seashore wildlife sanctuaries
smothering in oil from sinking tankers,
or an Indochinese village disappearing
in an orange ball of napalm, or a lake
dying from the mills in Buffalo,
or the slums of Baltimore.

I will not cry for Nimimosha:
St. Helens is the throat of Mother Earth,
and the violence is Her song—
and there is no sadness in it.

THE GRIM ART OF TEACHING

Don't look at me
with those woman's eyes
and that burgeoning womanhood bursting
out of clothes just made
for walking into classrooms:
Stop the show! Who cares
about Shakespeare, anyway?

Don't smile, don't stare, don't
tell me I'm cute, and don't make jokes
about meeting after school
that don't sound funny.

I'm damned near old enough
to be your father;
you're damned near old enough
to be my lover;
this is one damned dangerous way
to make a living.

MATTERS OF THE HEART

(for Thomas McGrath & James Cooney)

Old Tom, your rasping low voice
is so soft it's hard to imagine machine gun
bullets among the strikers in New Orleans
or the hard clubs on soft round heads
by the docks in New York City;
Jim shuffling along with your walking stick
like an angry shepherd, kind as a good Samaritan,
first American printer of Miller and Nin:

"The deepest part of a man is his sense
of essential truth, essential honour, essential
justice: they hated him because he was free,
because he wasn't cowed as they were... "

"Wild talk, and easy enough now to laugh.
That's not the point and never was the point:
What was real was the generosity, expectant hope.
The open and true desire to create the good."

You rascals. What am I supposed to do?
Storm the White House? Picket Chase Manhattan?
What? I've tried it all, believe me; nothing
works. Everyone's asleep, or much too busy.

The point is: things are different now.
In the age of the MX missle and the Trident
nuclear submarine and the 20-megaton bomb
multiplied by a couple of thousand or so,
what are the odds I'll ever see
the same age you are now?

Did it seem so bleak in 1940
in that awful twilight when half the world
plunged headlong into darkness
out of the decade of comradeship and hope
while the other half stood poised to follow?

Four more decades have passed since then,
and you're still at it. The Pole Star's gone;
even the dreams we steered by only ten years ago
are gone. Where do you get your strength?

I'm tired of being swatted like a bothersome fly:
pariah, voice in the wilderness. My friends
look at me with pity in their eyes.
I want to own a house, raise a family,
draw a steady paycheck. What, after all, can I do
to change the course of a whole mad world?

I'm only a man; I want to forget for awhile
and be happy. . .
                               . . .and yet your lives,
your words, your breath, your beating
old tired fighters' unbowed hearts
boom through the stillness of excuses
like a stuck clock forever tolling:

"Don't give in. Go on. Keep on.
Resist. Keep on. Go on."

BRIANA

(for CJ, in memory of Jill)

Death comes knocking and the silence descends
like a black bird alighting on the windowledge
on a black night with no candles.

Yet everything continues: bottle time,
nap time, play time, bath time, story time,
bed time—only a brief confusion:
for a few days you asked for mommy;
then you stopped asking.

You can't know the black bird will sit
for a lifetime in your father's heart.
I watch him with you now:
the tall slender frame
bending over your crib like a willow;
the large hands hesitantly poised—
wanting to touch,
not wanting to wake you;
the soft searching eyes permanently puzzling
an incomprehensible absence
he will never let you feel
if he can help it.

Years will pass before you understand
the secret tremble when your father holds you,
just how much such a small child weighs—
but that's okay;

                  don't trouble your dreams
with wondering. Be what you are:
your mother's daughter. Be a candle.

Light the awful silence with your laughter.

and other poems

LAUREL SPEER

DON'T DRESS YOUR CAT IN AN APRON

Don't dress your cat
in an apron.
Don't put your dog
in a hat.
Don't stick a leash
on your lizard,
or booties on your rat.

And don't,
most especially
Ms. disappointed America,
stick your stillborn baby
in the closet
wrapped in a blanket.

THE FAT ORANGUTAN

The orangutan on page 43
  is a famous one
in the annals of zoos.
Overfed for twenty years
by the best intentioned
hand of the populace,
it sits obese in captivity.
Grotesque jowls
and rolling paunch
render it inert
and strangely human
in its overlook.

THE DYING HAVE SAD EYES

*T*he family dog fails badly.
　　His hips will not hold his weight.
He crouches after his walk,
his feet splay
and he yelps if you touch his jaw.
Surely he is terminal
and kindness dictates
a quick and painless death.
This is permitted with pets.
But like our leukemic aunt,
we watch him waste
and hope that one day
when we wake up
he will be gone
and relieve us
of the burden of our choice.

DISPENSING JUSTICE UTTERLY

The camper got in his car
    to head home,
heard an ominous rustle
and found a 4 ft. rattler
coiled under his dash.

The motorist called the cops,
who flushed the reptile out
with a fire extinguisher,
shot his head off,
took him back to the station,
skinned him,
fileted him,
fried him in butter and ginger,
then ate him entirely up.

Delicious, smacked the killer cops,
dispensing justice
utterly.

EASTER RABBIT

The Easter rabbit
  has come
with a basket
of fecund eggs
and miniature snapshots
of centerfold legs
to wonder over
in celebration of spring,
when grass blades
erupt overnight
and the naked, baby birds
fall from their nests under eaves
and dry on cement
like worms after rain.
Regeneration is pock-marked
with death.
One out of every six
doesn't make it.
Puppies,
children,
goats,
calves.
The Easter rabbit himself,
like Lassie,
has been replaced
a dozen times
since he began.

MORE THAN WE PAID FOR

We sat in the first row.
    The nightclub entertainer
had this 7 ft. boa
wrapped around his neck,
when suddenly
the man seemed to miss
his reflexes.
The snake sensed his hesitation
and tightened down.
Someone screamed,
the victim turned blue,
the owner called the cops.
A spectator in the 5th row
tried to pry loose
those obdurate folds,
but it was no use.
Even after they cut off
the snake's head
to gasps of the audience,
it was clear the performer was dead,
which was more than we paid for
at the door.

LOOK AT THAT DEAD TROUT

The brown trout
  is pictured starey-eyed dead
by a creel,
fiberglass pole and reel,
pristine mountain scape
in soft focus background.

This is posed
as something beautiful,
something clean,
something all American to do.

As a kid,
pulling fingerlings
from a stream,
I had no reservations, either
watching their iridescent skins
turn worn nickle silver
gasping their last in air,
straight from there
to the pan,
gutted, glaze-eyed
corpses in cornmeal.

AT THE DESERT MUSEUM

*T*he prairie dogs
  refuse to come out and play.
Their village stands
all weeds and hillside
and we wonder if they're dead.
Some witless curator
has placed a family of Mexican wolves
next to the mule deer
and they pace and pace
and are tortured by proximity.
A single black bear slumps in the heat
in a cement corner,
looking like a moth-eaten rug,
refusing to turn his face
to the crowd,
blocked by a steep declivity.

School children
with identifying tags
as arcane as the names of the cactus
they stare at uncomprehendingly,
shift from foot to foot
while a teacher lectures
the wonder of a wren's nest.

A tourist motions us ahead
to cross his picture field,
saying he has all the time
in the world,
while a C. P. in a chair
gesticulates randomly,
carried from cage to cage
by a solicitous aunt,
locked in his own world
as much as any slit-eyed armadillo.

BRAINING THE CAT & OTHERS

*T*here's a certain hostility toward barking dogs
  we don't understand.
Poisoned meat thrown over walls
at mixed breed shepherds
who howl at fire trucks,
bits of hambuger clamped between convulsed jaws.
A twenty-two shell crushes a skull
coming from somewhere close by
unidentified.
Letters written on lawyer's stationery
threatening to sue
unless the nuisance is deposed to silence
by operations on vocal cords.

There's a certain hostility toward cats
we don't understand, either.
Those well mannered, silent creatures
peering owlishly from hiding places
between leaves.
One was brained by a shovel
then buried in a shallow hole
scooped out by blue-veined hands
of the shuffling lady next door.
The exhumed corpse
examined by a vet
determined a blow
from a blunt instrument did that cat in.

The lady in question says
So what?
You gonna sue?

We're concerned for our children
playing in alleys,
barking like dogs,
hiding like cats.
We tell them to beware thrown meat,
glinting barrels caught off reflections
from windows,
the snuffling, squint-eye next door
gripping her blunt instrument
in arthritic fingers.

SULPHUROUS SMOKE ROLLS OUT OF HELL

Sulphurous smoke pours from my mouth.
   I flail for breath.
My foot strikes flint, throwing off sparks,
hardens to keratin,
going cloven before my locked eye.
A tail sprouts behind,
switches with glee at its autonomy.
I reach up to touch my cheek
and find skin scaled
as tight as alligator hide
on shoes or handbag.

This is worse than Pinocchio braying ass
at missing school.
Extinguish the light.
Lucifer pounds my temples,
eyes glowing like stove coals
to get out.

WINDOWS
AND
WALLS

poems by

RICHARD JONES

for Kate

The greatest writer cannot see through a
brick wall but, unlike the rest of us, he
does not build one.
    —W. H. Auden, *The Dyer's Hand*

THE BELL

In the tower the bell
is alone, like a man
in his room,
thinking and thinking.

The bell is made of iron.
It takes the weight
of a man
to make the bell move.

Far below, the bell feels
hands on a rope.
It considers this.
It turns its head.

Miles away,
a man in his room
hears the clear sound,
lifts his head to listen.

GRAVEYARD

Moonlight is turning everything blue.
A blue mist rises from the fields.
You feel your soul leaving your body
like a scarf pulled from a pocket.
You would halo the moon,
but the earth is soft,
your body is heavy,
and a hand is writing your name
on the unmarked stone.

THE LETTER

The clerk in the post office stops
one minute, lays down
a handful of letters on the table.
The wall of wooden letter slots waits.

He removes his glasses and wipes them
with ahandkerchiefpulled from his pocket.
When he breathes on the glass,
he can see the fingerprint of the world.

As he cleans his glasses he thinks
of his son, of the boy's last letter,
the casual way he wrote,
"I go back to the front."

The red hand circles the face of a giant clock.
Today the country is at peace.
He begins to read; each envelope
bears the name of a stranger.
Each minute it begins again.

He holds the letter in his hand,
feels it moving through the world
breathless and white.

DISHRAGS

After our last meal
these worn-out dishrags
will clean the empty plates.

Then, as long as we live, we'll wear
dishrags in our breastpockets.
We'll comfort each other. Like gentlemen
we'll flourish dishrags
when our famished women begin to weep.

We'll march off elegantly
in front of the guns.
We'll be so hungry our eyes will grow.
We'll look like a troupe of skinny dancers.
They're going to have to shoot us to keep us
from waving dishrags over our heads.

And should we make it,
should any one of us live to build
the new city
where everyone has enough,
we'll dry our dishrags on clotheslines,
window to window.

Dishrags will fly like flags
reminding us of our hunger and our hope.

CELEBRATE THE WALLS

It's impossible for me
to celebrate the walls
we've made between ourselves.

There are a hundred million people
on the other side of the window.

Some of them have gone crazy,
their spirits killed
so only their bodies keep moving.

Some lives are a great sadness
no one can penetrate.

A few are a bad miracle,
a trick for making money.

And walls built up between. . . .

I'll celebrate the walls
when they're knocked down,
the walls that have crumbled
into a mountain of bricks.

We'll climb right up to the top
so God and his businessmen
will have to look us in the face.

THE EXECUTION

Hands tied behind my back
I must look like a man
with something very important
to remember: what have I done?
I have loved my wife,
kissed my son each morning
while he was still asleep,
sunlight falling on his face.
The sun now on my face,
the rough bricks of the wall
scratching my back, my heart
beating like a drum so loud
I can't hear anymore, I see
someone laugh because
my pants are wet. It's stupid
to think a blindfold could protect me
from eternity, or the soldiers
from my eyes. I don't want it.
I want to see everything,
how it took me a lifetime to learn
to leave my dream, to get out
of bed and put on my shoes.
Hands behind my back, the last
cigarette between my teeth
pushed out at the soldiers

like a hot kiss, I remember
everything, the way
my wife threw me down on the grass,
how my son jumped on top of us,
his laughter loud as guns.

THE SPIDERS

It took my father and me years to learn
how to talk. Now we don't say anything.
We touch each other from a distance,
two men carrying a ladder
we set against his house.

Along the coast, people live
in houses built on stilts,
so when storms rage up the shore
the ocean passes safely underneath.

Spiders live there, too,
working their webs each day.
In one evening
they can cover the house
while he's inside, sleeping,
sprawled across the bed
as though he'd fallen there by accident
to finish the day.

When I visit my father,
we cover our faces with rags.
We mix poison. I can't turn away,
holding the ladder so my father doesn't fall,

and this helps me understand,
this is what we always needed,
a common enemy and poison,
something we could do that meant something,
something to forgive and something to kill,
so I forgive everything,
I forgive my father and I forgive myself,
and I don't turn away from the spiders
or the holy water poison silently blessing this house.

BREAD CRUMBS

They knock with their Bibles
on your grandmother's front door.
One man presses his fat red face
against the screen, yelling,

but he can't see you. The two of you
are a secret behind the sofa.
It's a little game:
when a salesman comes
you play silence and hiding and no money.

Your grandmother knows the virtue of patience.
The man on the porch will go away.
So you wait like a child, head bowed,
for a prayer to end, when all you want

is to eat supper with her,
and afterwards, sweep the table clean
the way she showed you,
one hand brushing bread crumbs into the other—

both hands filled,
just enough in each fist to open
the door and face the hungry day.

LOVE IS A FALL
FROM GRACE

What good is talking?
We give words destinations
but they always take the wrong turn.
They wander down empty backstreets
at night, suspicious characters
mumbling to themselves.

When I really want to talk,
you understand best
the old wooden chair
smashed in an argument,
a fistful of flowers still blooming
in the sake bottle on the window ledge
long after they should have been dead.

But love is another language.
That's three days without talking,
three days without sex,
then twenty minutes naked in the apple orchard,
your mouth eating the words
that come falling out of mine.

POEM FOR KATE

The world goes on forever.
Forever I've loved you.
While you sleep
I stand outside in the night,
feel where the sun burned my back,
the darkness like a cool balm.

Tonight I'm lonesome and happy.
As I walk along, I feel
a sentimental attachment to the earth,
to the lake, and to the wind
which sounds like rain
as it rustles the leaves.

Hear that dog howling two farms away?
That's me, chained to the earth.

I want this poem carved in stone,
a little haiku
repeating its song in the meadow—

Why am I happy?
In a million years I'll be
standing here with you.

PETALS
FROM
THE
WOMANFLOWER

poems by

Margaret Key Biggs

for
Gini, Mila, Becky, Barbara

CALICO CARIBES

In small towns,
gossipers gather
as fast as storm clouds
when a scandal emerges
like Grendel's mother
from the depths of a pool,
a monster seeking flesh;
not until they have cleaned
each victim's bones
with piranha skill
do they return to their homes
where they hide sins
as black as obsidian stones
in spotless white cupboards.

EARTH MUSIC

She is over sixty
and goes to the beach every day,
for it is the only place
she can wear few clothes
and lie upon the earth
to listen to its natural rhythms;
the girl within the wrinkled skin
has never lost her lust
for earth music.

❧ UNDER THE MUSHROOM

I smelled the politician's promises
singed and burned
into malodorus black crows
flying over fetid fields.

I heard the wind whistle
through my father's bones
dried beneath the fire bush
that stole its color from the sun.

I saw my mother's flesh
fall from her face
as if it had been fire-cut
by Dark-age dragons.

I tasted the last possible kiss
before my lover's lips
melted into the past
that would know no future.

I felt the unbelievable heat
sear my screaming soul
as it curled into a shadow
to linger forever on concrete steps.

✦ STERN WARNING

if a woman does not
drive the creeblesteps away,
keep the packiwogs at bay,

if she fails to flush
the bittletraps from their nest,
along with cittersnaps and the rest,

if she is careless about
the thundersnouts upstream
or chokibouts that steal dreams,

if she dares to forget
wunderwittles up so high
and berriskittles in the sky,

then she will become
the slave of dwiddleclutches
or the mistress of swiddlewutches.

IN SEARCH OF A SECOND DAWN

She can willingly forgive him
for losing his luster,
for wilting under the sun,

but she can never absolve him
for losing his enthusiasm,
for making her feel old;

she knows a woman withers
without scintillation in her life,
that his heart has become a moonscape

reflecting the light stolen from the sun.
That is the exact moment
she decides to look for a smile

that will refract her remaining light
into the rays of a second dawn
before darkness declares sovereignty.

SEASONED

Now I know
your bodyscape so well
that I can have you
riding on the carousel
and reaching for the golden ring
even before you have decided
you want to go to the fair.

THE EXCHANGE

Mumtaz was thirty-nine when she died
giving birth to her fourteenth child within eighteen years.
Shah Jehan built a monument of art to her:
    marble embroidery
        jewel script
            alabaster lace
                slender minarets
                    a massive spired dome
                        pietra dura *in perfection*
                          a reflection pool
a tomb twenty-two thousand men
spent twenty-two years of life to accomplish.
Art has always been the victim of war,
for even the master survivor, the Sphinx, shows evidence
of the guns of the Mamelukes,
but in 1803 when British cannonballs
threatened the perfection of the Taj Mahal,
the Hindus surrendered victory in exchange for beauty;
for once in history, art's power stopped war.

GIRL UNDER STREETLIGHT

She sagged against the streetlight
making an oval of yellow to hold her shadow;
even purse-snatchers and rapists
held back from the aura
of a woman with nothing to lose.
She ignored tears on her pale cheeks,
and said to me as I neared,
"There are things worse than death,"
then walked down Tennessee Street
to be swallowed by Tallahassee.

THE COUPLE

As old as they are,
he still looks fit;
she has wilted
into a wheelchair.
It is awkward
for her to eat;
she holds close
to her plate,

yet he took her
to her favorite place.
We who saw him
admired him,
his sense of duty.

When she finished,
he lifted her
to the chrome cradle.
He smiled into
her pale eyes,
and we saw

the perfection Pygmalion
prayed for Aphrodite to give,
and the love for which
Orpheus bargained Hell.

WOMAN UNTOUCHED

Her loneliness imprisons her
in a dark womb
unfed by umbilical hope.
Her skin cries for strokes
that will never come again;
the woman is dying from a hunger,
savage and searing and wilting,
the woman is dying.

AT EVE'S HOUSE

*I played with Eve
because she could scramble
the pear tree easier than I;
besides, she did not complain,
and there were many tears
around my childhood.
Once, I went to her house
whose wood was silver
from want of paint
through many seasons.
It was the neatest house
I had ever entered;
there wasn't much
to clutter it. Eve led me,
oh so carefully, to her room,
shut off from the rest,
an even more barren place,
but it was there we learned
to ignite purple imaginations
to transcend beige deserts
to find the mountain
where Pegasus freed
a stream from which
we continue to drink.*

FROM THE WOMANFLOWER

Since you know a cocoon
is a clinging promise
of butterfly,

and a chameleon changes color
with mood or need,
will lose one tail
to gain another,

that the top-heavy bumblebee
should not fly
but does,

an oyster is male one year
and female the next,

why do you say
my dreams are nonsense
merely because they are petals
from the womanflower?

PHILIPPE AT HIS BATH

a poem by

Constance Pierce

*H*e stands, naked
Except for his socks,
In the middle of the room,
Ears rushing
With the faucet's blast,
History—suddenly on him
Like a summer fever.
To will a calm, perhaps
(By luck) to fool himself,
He assumes the pose
Of sanguine muser:
Stroking his chins
Where a scattered stubble
Instantly pleasures
His palm, gives some
Relief. He cannot keep
His hand from edging down—
Oh, just a curd's worth!
To where the whiskers
Give way to an infant
Smoothness
The texture of custard.

132

*A*s a boy in France,
In the stern little town
Where he had been
Schooled with a horde
Of masturbators, students
Of catholic history
(And weird Bataille,
Covert), he had been
A purveyor of sweets—
Tartes sucrées, des demoiselles tatin,
Religieuses and *savarins*—
Procuring them from the confectioner
And the forbidden cupboard
Of the old woman from whom
His Father (the Bastard)
Had rented him a room.
Toad without, fox within,
He would offer his delights
To the wildest boys, the brutes
Of the upper forms, watch
Them cram their pink faces,
Greedy and oblivious to him,
His own face crammed—all lost
In a silent orgy
Of spewing crumbs and honeyed dribble.

*N*ow, disconsolate
To find himself
The curator of an ill-endowed museum
In the American West, he subscribes
To Cheesecake-of-the-Month,
Hordes tins of *marrons-glacés*,
Stands patient at the stove
In his bland apartment
(High above the frightful Plain)
In the middle of the night
And stirs fudge, dropping
Walnuts into its warm swirl
With dextrous fingers.

*N*ow his belly burgeons
Like a ball of helium,
Barely tethered
To his ribs. Beneath,
His scrotum drips
(Soft and discolored . . .
Like a too-ripe fig)

*A*t school,
In the old woman's house,
He had ravaged again
(And again!) the irresistible
Cushion
On a fat, puce-colored
Chair, leaving his mark
Beneath a doily of dusty lace.
Later, there had been
A boy
A few years older
Than himself (beautiful
And slow-
Witted, infatuated).
In the afternoons,
When the others mouthed
Prayers and poetry
In the common room,
The two of them
Had huddled in a crypt-
Like cell beneath: stroking
The rubbery prongs, the shapes
Of heat in the dark—with love
On the dim boy's part,
Mournful . . . inarticulate.

As for himself, lost
In the moist absence
Of light, he became
A flying squish
Of blood and gluten. Above,
The mock-pious voices droned.
Heels were scuffed
In a shameless rhythm
The two villains rushed
To match. Finally
They burst. The odor
Of dead mice
Drilled his nostrils.

*A*t night, back
In the old woman's house
Where his Father
(The Meddler, the Son
Of a Bitch) had sought
To keep him pure,
He raped the long sausage-
Shaped pillow on his bed,

Throwing the hussy
Roughly on her back,
Straddling the tube of her body,
Chafing his parts
Against the starched casing.
"Whore," he whispered,
Voice like static.
"Take that. And that."

*T*oo nervous to shave,
He pulls off his socks,
Stepping on the toe
Of each in turn, extracting
A foot. He moves
Toward the tub where
His bathwater bubbles with oil
And sinks in, settles
Back. Willing a smile
To hoist the mass
Of chins. The horror
Of the earth, stretching
(Flat and   vicious)
Into the night, begins
To fall away. He forgets

Troublesome history, forgets
For a moment the miserable
Little museum with its odor
Of rat turds, its pathetic
Diptychs peeling, its
Third-rate tableaux, even
Its one good piece: God
Sternly rendered
By an unknown Fra
(Long dust, yes,
In the golden fields of Tuscany);
Locked in a bank vault
Now, wanting his decision—
Prompting ulcers
As he ponders daily
(Going along the low walls—
Like the lowest caretaker!—
Sweeping up debris
The crumbling junk
Has shed like snakeskin
As he slept): Where
To hang the thing?

*O*h, in his bath
These problems fade. They
And the fearsome Chicanos
Who lean whispering against walls
As he—skulks!—home
In the evening: they
And the silly cowboys
In their hats and spurs, bucking
Through the streets, high
At the wheels of their Broncos.

*T*he soap beneath his hand
Glides on the Hindenburg
Of his stomach
Like *crème anglaise* . . .

*D*uring the War,
His family had made a pudding
Of mother's milk, his own
Mother paying the girl,
The daughter of the farmhand,
A few francs
To squeeze it in a bottle.

The girl had brought it,
Blue and creamless,
To the back door, tucked
The money into her apron
Pocket, and never looking up,
Had scooted back across the field.
At night, while their fields
Were plundered by soldiers and
Resistance, he would drown
Out the harsh sounds
With the drip, drip, drip
Of the girl's milk, filling
His head with her: the nipple
Tortured between the scissors
Of her fingers: the large
Blue globules spurting, finally
Running like a river
Into the cavern of his glass.

*W*hen the war was over,
Before they left their farm—
His mother and sisters for Paris,
He for his final year at school—
He had met the girl

At night in the stable,
And lying her down
In front of the window,
Had opened her dress—stared
At the creamless flesh in the moonlight:
Swollen and taut as aspic,
She being pregnant again. . . .

*E*yes slitted by memory, he rubs
The slick soap in circles
On his belly, chanting
Softly: "jo, jo, jo."

*T*he wash-cloth floats by
His leg, breaking his reverie
With its rough cat's tongue.
He picks it up and rubs it
Against his cheek. It has
The feel of wartime wool.

When the soldiers had come
Those last days in Paris
Before his Father
(The electricity mogul,
The Power, the Light)
Had sent the family to
The country, set about
A Vichy compromise—
There had been a glamour
In the square uniforms,
The polished boots and brass
That compelled a boy
To a deep, if silent
Respect. Like steel
They moved, the soldiers:
Stiff, erect.
And in his dreams
He wore their trim jackets,
Their firm set of lip.

Months later
In the country, he heard
A woman from the village
Croak out to his mother

A tale: an old man
Had refused gas
To the soldiers, had been
Forced to drink
Water, litres of
Water, an endless stream of
Water, the woman had said,
Wall-eyed, stalled
In the word. Then they
Had lain him in the road,
Jumped on his stomach,
Burst him. "He vomited
Green . . . and red,"
The woman had sobbed
Into the sleeve of her sweater.

*C*rouching behind the pantry door,
He breathed in the reek
Of old wool and felt sick.
But he could not connect
The geyser of Christmas vomit
With the crisp soldiers
In their belted jackets,
Their blazing boots.

*A*s for Jews,
He did not know any
At the time.

*W*hen the photographs
Had finally come,
When he had seen
The wraiths, the proof
Looking out from pulpy
Magazines, he had wanted
To go with food,
Large dishes of berries
And cream, to spoon these
Into the scorched mouths
And cradle the hairless
Skulls in the fleece
Of his jacket.

*B*ut there were so many.

In the end, he had wanted
To cover them all, plow
Swiftly with a bulldozer
And bury the evidence
In the earth—

"O Earth, O tortured,
Tortured Earth," he wrote
One spring day in a
Tortured burst of poetry,
Looking across the fields
That stretched to Belsen
From the little town
Where his school half-
Remained, a wing intact
Amid the free-standing walls
And jags where windows had been.
The old woman was gone
And her house
With its succulent chair—
The boy, too: Dead
In the bombing of Liege,

Someone had said.
"Your heart is bored
With maggots. But you
Put on your green dress
To pleasure fools. Shit
It out, Earth! Blow
The filthy mess
Beyond the stars!"

*I*n a year, his Father
(The Brute, the Authority
In absentia) was dead, jammed
Into the earth with the rest,
And he, poetry behind him,
Hiked across the vine-striped hills
Along the Nahe, drank beer
In *Rathäuser* and on terraces
Under great red umbrellas
Where he watched American
Soldiers piss in the geraniums,
Their silly little jackets
Askew, slipped up over
Their wrinkled shirts, hats
Gliding across their heads
Like canoes.

Along the roads, the Germans—
Civilians now—roared
On motorcycles, their heads
Bullet-shaped in sleek leather
Caps, their jaws bold
And firm beneath the black
Disks of their goggles.
All the green stillness
Of those afternoons
Was sucked into the great
Motors: held, controlled,
Then released in an unrepentent
Bellow, lingering long
After the engines had passed
Him at his beer.
In the sidecars,
Young women in tight
White sweaters coolly rubbed
The leather of their gloves
Into the webs of their fingers,
Never looking up.

*A*t night, in the soft down
Beds of Bad Kreuznach
And Bingen, he dreamed:
Of the soldiers
And himself
Ringing the geraniums,
The soldiers laughing,
Tugging their prongs out
Of their woolen flies,
He—grinning and silent,
Fiddling with his buttons,
Urine and earth sloshing
Onto his shoes; and then:
The soldiers, laughing,
Their pricks
Circumcized and mounted
On shafts of bone, drowning
The geraniums in the fallout
From their steady arcs of blood.
His own penis
In his hand now, its head
Capped in leather, its eye
Glowing red behind dark goggles.

$\mathcal{I}$n the fall, he went to America.

$\mathcal{I}$n a university of cinderblock
Gothic, he would study religious
Art of the Middle Ages
And early Renaissance.

$\mathcal{H}$e slips his hand,
Water-soaked and fluted,
Beneath his thigh and bounces
The walnuts, tweaks the acorn,
Spreads his square fingers
Wide to enclose the whole
Nutty apparatus
In a tepid clasp.
Oh, there had been women,
Yes. Their legs open
To his rocket, soaring
To probe the moons
And stars and planets
Of their vast black space,
"Shot his wad,"
As the Americans say.
"Big oaks from little acorns grow."

And how they had displeased
Him, after all, with their
Quick trips to the toilet,
Their peeing diseases,
Their miserable periods,
Always late—held off untill
He had fretted himself
Into a state. Oh, but how
He had punished them
With his silences, wrapping
Himself in his robe
And sitting stern as a monk
Over a rare text, filling
The air with the most subtle
Beethoven. And when their fury
Reached its limits, when
Their eyes and lips quivered
Like junket, like mousse . . .
He would give the knife
An ingenious twist, call
His estranged wife,
The Jew—
Greet her with a jam-sauce
Of endearments, of tender
Accents and chuckles,
Pecking the receiver
With playful kisses.

And when the girls
Had cried, had drawn themselves
Into their heart-
Breaking spheres of sorrow,
He would relent:
Go to them,
Pull them into his robe
And pat their hair.
It was good for them
To suffer. It made him
Love them all the more, be
Tolerant of their irritating
Ways.

Finally, he would bend them
Over a chair, move
Dog-like against them,
Trembling near tears
At the sight of their pale
Cheeks lifted toward him,
Their poor legs straining. . . .

*A*n errant foot dislodges
The stopper from the drain,
And he springs up from
His reverie, whisking
Himself above the water,
Saving once again that
Door to his being
From the prehensile devils
That live barely under the surface
Of his chosen, his com-
Promised land. Diminished,
He steps from the tub,
The buoyant ambergris of his lost
Desire becoming
Tangled in leg-hair. Abstracted
And, suddenly, depressed—
He scours himself with the towel,
Digging in between the buttocks,
Worrying the puckered emblem
Of the Truth: *Je suis un cul.*
An asshole. Why had they
Left him, all the little girls
With the white hips, his wife,
The comforting burden, the Jew
Whom he had masked with his safe
Name? Dropping the towel

On the hamper, he heads
Toward his kitchen. He
Would take a morsel of something,
A baked pear, a little cake
Perhaps. Tomorrow . . .
What the hell? He would hang
The Fra's picture
In his rat's hole
Of an office, place it
Flush with his chair.
Why not? He and the Father
Would settle in cozy as corpses,
Stare into each other's eyes
As vision decomposed, every moment
A blinding High Noon . . .

That would take care of it.

ROBBING THE PILLARS

poems by HARRY HUMES

for Nancy

☐ Robbing the Pillars

"Pillars were columns of coal
left standing as supports
for the mine tunnel."

Nervousness of eye and ear,
air like slate in my mouth,
pick and shovel heavy near fingers.
A half mile above, the mountain is green.
There are children, a woman,
the house with bright rooms.

Often in veins of coal
I have imagined sighs of the dying
cut off and at the last
eating wood and leather belts,
sulphur water turning their eyes ashen
with dreams of angels.

Carbide coats the chambered air,
buggies rattle narrow gangways.
My father was here years ago.
One by one, I rob the pillars he left,
haul coal away, watch the ceiling,
remember cool tiles of kitchens.

■   ■

The tunnel creaks with bones,
brittle syllables, bad lungs.
Each hour passes like swamps turning carbon.
In the town, children clap hands.
The woman hears tons of balance
slipping from green plant to dark fossil,

and hears me as I begin, slowly,
to rise along a cable of light.
I have broken atoms of gravity
and will feel at my wrist all night long
hollows of blood, the great void breathing,
the tap, tap, tap of a last message on stone.

☐ Photographs of Men, Dogs and Foxes at Stine's Corner

My eye catches
on the photograph's assortment
of guns, hats, faces, hunting jackets on
    chairs,
the five hounds and three dead foxes
all neatly arranged against
the heavy black and white planes.
I lean into the scene
of late autumn below hardwood ridges
and breath becoming crystals.
I listen for sounds deep in the fur of animals
and try to imagine walking down a hill
into the day of the photograph
and standing there like a father or brother
of men who hunt, who become pictures
on walls of crossroads hotels.

My eyes look away into the ends of August
where a farmer cuts his alfalfa
and a blonde girl rides her bicycle.
It's so long ago the dogs howled after foxes

■   ■

and the men turned,
after walking red-faced from the woods,
turned into photographs and then sat
at round tables of dark beer and smoke,
their stories rising and falling
around them like seasons.

I listen to all of them
as I walk to the wooden porch
that gathers late light like a face at a wide
      window.
So the year poses its fields and edges of
      woods
around me exactly as I remember,

though I cannot say now whether the foxes
were red or gray, or whether the men
were anything more than stiff ceremonies
of November.

■   ■

☐ The Master of Dirt

Nothing about him is green or blue,
deep caves hang close to his eyes.
All day long, a chill rattles hands and feet,
the spade of his words goes deeper than ever.
His coming changes the roots of the year.
All these seasons, he has made
the small rooms smaller,
the faces more what they never were.

January and the windows
have little heat and no answers.
I hear him digging past rain and snow,
entering wrist and small patch of blood.

There are no phrases for such fierce
    emptiness,
for what causes the ground
to resemble a single face
I try over and over to forget.

■　　■

☐ The Deacon's Arm

The way he walked up our street—
the swing of his new arm
of leather, wood, and hooked steel.
He'd strap it on like a gangster's rig
to shoulder and chest.
When I was eleven, he let me wear it.
And when he died, it hung in our attic
for years near shotguns and magazines.
One day, it wasn't there.

Now from the blue chair
I watch the season's veins move downward
to root-ends and limestones
and I think of him,
how hundreds of feet underground
his real arm disappeared
in a tunnel of blue fire,
how his world must have tilted
forever out-of-balance for him.

■　■

I can feel beneath the chair
the roll of Mammoth and Buck and Orchard,
all the dark veins flowing
past lost arms and lives,
skeletal fingers still locked on shovels
or scratching on rock.

Nearby are fields and autumn sun,
a firmness of surface.
The room's timbers do not hold up the
    earth.
Nothing dynamites the garden
nor crashes down from the walls
to flood chambers of eye or mouth,
though in the steady drilling of years,
the blue-scarred faces remain.
The rocks crash down, the sirens still wake,
and the Deacon walks restlessly past me. . .
Father, Uncle, Brother in a world
made of leather and wood and steel,
and my blood falls precisely toward all of it,
toward the arm at the center.

■ ■

☐ Coal Pickers

In this wilderness of yellow leaves
and constellations burning
above our rooms in the spilled distances
    of air,
I think of them in their sad weathers
closing doors behind them at dawn,
walking an alley toward railroad and mine
    road.

They stop for breath by mountain laurel
or spill bank, day beginning to glow
near fossil; maybe they touch slate
or stir dark pools with sticks.
If they are women they have babushkas
tied to their heads; if they are men,
the simple hats of the village.

All day long they move down ridge,
fingers curling like sunspots around pieces
    of coal.
Do they feel old motions of swamp

or giant fern beneath white birch and
    chicadee?
Or hot against their palms a killing ice,
great bones staggering one morning,
the smoldering silence of another?

I sit now in my own slow ashen dusk
and hear feet scraping shale or old timber.
What they whisper near the old tunnel's
    clammy air
is what I have remembered for years.
I turn with them as they turn toward home,
their rattling buckets filled,
the northern sky around them like cold
    grates.

☐ The Last Miner Is Found

1.

The others have been carried
through smoke to the surface
the faces waiting
in the blue afternoon

                    but this one
waits with his back against cribbing
his bare head to his chest

2.

He was the first on the vein's face
the one who saw the timber splitting
or felt the air still
before the tunnel sucked at him
blew his eyes shut
even before he could yell out

He has been sitting there
these three days
                    like someone waiting
for pigeons to come in at evening

Now he is the last to be wrapped in white
and placed gently in the gunboat
and carried upward to the small point
of light that falls toward his stiff face
like the cruelest of cave-ins

■   ■

□ A Cold Condition

Fingers stiff, shoulders caved-in,
the mountains with their emptiness,
and someone walking beneath the maples.
I open doors, turn corners
past the stones of the day
and am chilly with the brass-handled
     landscape
that gathers like zero near collar and wrist.

Tomorrow when I stand by the silence
I've waited for year after year,
I'll remember equators
of basement, backyard coal bin, tool box,
the hands everywhere on my life.

A neighbor's clothes line
will flap its icy language.
There will be celery sticks,
small trays of leftovers.

All evening long
an old woman will go on looking
into all the corners of the room
for a warmer season.

■   ■

□ The Miners' Vacation

They come up out of the rockholes
and gangways past the pockets of gas,
lanterns swinging from belts,
lunch cans rattling as they step
out of the gunboats into the ribbed light
falling past laurel and huckleberry bush.

They will ride the surface for two weeks
    like corks,
and gather near corners testing noon light
for cracks or turning at a sound behind them
like fuses burning down.

At evening beneath the circling pigeons
they will tell their small sons
               Do not
follow us ever do not come down
to where water and blue fire
wait behind walls or underfoot
to break loose near shovel or pick
to rise days later smoking and swirling
with more white messages
Do not put on black rubber boots

And wake each dawn
thinking of treacherous Furnace Slope,
ribs bending, pushing out,
the great slips gathering speed,
crushing timber down the Buck vein.

Think of them
in white linen pants and shirts,
white shoes, as their arms and faces turn
    brown
near sunny spill bank or wash dam.

Think of them walking past open doors,
of the songs they begin to hear
in such long days of light.

☐ All the Ways Back

All the way back I had been thinking
of how he stood near pigeons or mine shaft
or at the center of hounds
and felt I could have walked
past the hickory, over the mountain again
to his hands, voice,
the way he wore his hat.

But now I think of crocus and bud,
air nervous with blackbird and gull,
the dead muskrat settling lower
lower over its bones.

Out there
a neighbor enters his barn,
a child plays behind the stone house,
the wind bell quiet. . .

Christ, the names, white dresses,
the path over the mountain,
the velvet hair of women,
faces at doorway or window,
Christ, all the ways back precisely
    remembered.

□ Walking the Anthracite

It could be the rim of the world,
the rocks breathing summer,
the copperheads coiled brilliant
near the huckleberry bushes.
Below me, there could be a town,
row homes like teeth set too close together,
dust on all the windows.
And then there's the ravine with the small
    pool,
smells of ferns, birch, the wet undersides
of last year's leaves, the musk of last night's
    beasts.
There's an old coal mine, its tipple rotting,
tunnels caved-in for hundreds of feet
and wires strewn everywhere, cans of nails
rusting beside the old shack.
There used to be a man here, a father
with bad lungs and scar-blue knees.
I imagine him standing at his pit, the earth
thick on him, eyes gathering

all the light before he went down.
This ground could be my darkest blood,
its hot veins places I must crawl.
I think of my wife, her pregnant shape.
I am mined by fatherhood; I have broken my
      carbons,
dynamited my flesh, walked alone into these
      hills for days.
At night, by an old carbide lamp,
drinking the bitter hill water,
I feel the tunnels rising like charms to my
      flesh,
calming me, offering the lost pale face like
      long sleep.

■   ■

MENTIONING
DREAMS

MICHAEL RATTEE

ADASTRA PRESS
EASTHAMPTON, MA
1985

Sleeping Among Birds

If when you close your eyes
You follow the two stars that replace them
Into the darkness where your body
Becomes a fragment of heaven
What you've been unable all day to remember
Will be the sounds that only seem to wake you
As your dreams become something
Of which you are certain

And in the morning laughing
About having slept among birds
You'll notice the sound of chirping
In your wife's laughter
Swinging your legs out of bed your feet
Will land in a pile of feathers where
Last night you had left your clothes
You'll begin finding the straws
That you carry out of your sleep
And with them you will begin lining
Your nest of worries asking
Yourself all day what it is you've forgotten

The Expected Night

(for my wife)

A sudden wind in cold weather
Turned us into birds
That's the reason we nest
In this warm climate
Working our quiet song
Into the expected night
Each note reaches further in the dark
Towards a silence that is not sleep
But is the sound of ourselves
Waking in that place where we are each alone

Reinventing Light

As a child I believed the birds
Reinvented light every morning
And during the day
It was slowly turned into ink
For the night to write stories with
I believed that until I was taught
It was all mechanics
And stories were written by people
Mostly older than ourselves
Some so old they couldn't be photographed
My teachers explained everything
But left the sadness out of it
That has remained with me
And this morning I watched the night
Run out of ink again and the birds
Come to inspect what was written

Discovering Hands

(for Michael Anthony Rattee)

Before me stood a pale forest
At the edge of which villagers hardening
    with age
Were foraging things from the air
Smiling hesitantly I approached them
And was immediately offered a small bird to eat
It felt alive and a pulsing entered my mouth
Everything I'd seen until then became
    unimportant
I discovered that what I touched I could name
And my tongue remains a wing struggling in
    the wind

Grade School} A Daydream of Birds

The teacher is saying something about
The geography and population of the Mid-west
While you recall last Sunday
Your friend had six chicks in a cloth bag
Starlings you thought
A name too lovely for scavengers
He said they were grackles anyway
And began beating the corner of the barn
With a repeated and weakening chirping
The bag began to resemble a limp bouquet
And you stood absolutely still
Holding a lilac blossom and watching a
        hummingbird
Repeatedly make itself disappear
Wondering at the chances of that bird
Colored like oil on water
Appearing in your hand
Whispering it's beautifully alive
Nothing at all like the death of flowers

The Moderns

When you were twelve years old
The scenery on that river was so beautiful
It was like going by boat
From one dream to the next
The first brave girls
Springing up bare breasted on the banks
Where after a kiss it was silent
A miracle in modern life
And you woke embarrassed in a stained bed
But to the moderns that isn't really living
They don't care that you remember
Being twelve and dreaming
What matters to them is what it costs you
They think closed eyes are a threat to youth
Even if morning appeared through mosquito
    netting
And the flat trees were full of monkeys
What they'd want to know is the components
    of light
And the 'scientific' name for vision
Their sense of things gets lost
At the mention of dreams
And they don't want to know you
Instead they call you by your first name
Or something even shorter
And point out the old people sleeping on the
    edge

A New Country

This is a room full of people
Who want to travel
Their breath leaves a trail of jet vapors

Most want to go home
But a few dream of a place
So different they need to describe it

A shore with no souvenirs
Where the surf shines its language
Long into the night

As the homebound recite their familiar names
These others' eyes fill with the sea
And their pockets bulge with wind

They are becoming a new country
Whose borders are carried inside them
Its history contained in each of their lives

German Dreams

The moon pulls at her sorrow
And she wakes surrounded by dreams
Of her mother's life
Of missing forests and *Tragikomödie*

So as not to laugh
She turns on the stove
Even with two oceans between them
She fears her mother would hear
Those misfortunes returning
And begin worrying all over again
Perhaps even forgetting
The thirty six years
Since the present was so terrible
She preferred going hungry
Riding a freight train from Breslau
With her four children since lost
By accident suicide drink and marriage
But really she would laugh
At her daughter's turning on the stove
As though to burn her German dreams
And worrying about the distance
Her laughter would travel

She would laugh while her tears
Like shimmering fragments found in the surf
Reminded her of oceans
Each of them containing a reason for laughing

Long Fingers

(for Reg)

My brother's piano was a dream of long
      fingers
Each night placing his hands under his pillow
He would wake from nightmares
More afraid of the dark than before

After a dream of his love dying in Guatemala
He gave up painting
And his desire for music became immense
His stubby fingers moved along the table edge
In the pattern of some breakfast concerto
Walking to class his hands conducted
A symphony among birds and weather

He believes he's outgrown the impulse
That pulling the hearts from automobiles
Has tamed his hands
But his wife knows when he strokes her breasts
They're the first two notes of a chorale
And his son's hair is an opera
That he's filled with a desire for music and
      long fingers

When Grandmother Died

The wind became an anger I walked into
Trying to remember her voice
As my arms raised and lowered
Clouds the color of tin roofs formed between
    them
In the shape of her profile
And the sounds of animals surrounded my
    heart
Clawing her stories from me

Intrigued by the possibilities of her own place
She had told me her dreams
Of the visible history of the air around us
Of stairways covered with centuries of sleep
Of birds with songs of coiled light
Secrets only I believed

Alone

(for my mother)

Nights you dream of a man with fingers
    like rain
Who holds in the palm of his hand
A place you have wanted to be
He speaks in the dual language of doors
But the words you recognize are the old ones
That sting your eyes like silence
As he walks away from you
Through a field lit by lightning
All night wanting to be alone
Leaving you listening to your heart ring
Like a bell left out in the rain

A Slow Tune

The air curls above mother's radio
As she dances alone to a slow tune
It is mid-morning and
What's left of her youth
Would like to move faster
For it to be Saturday with a dime in her pocket
But it's a song about love
And she knows not to rush it
Maybe this Saturday her husband
Will take her heart to the movies
And she'll thank him
By telling about this song she danced to
While his laughter turns her younger
And they'll walk slowly home singing it

Lawn Trees\If It's Not Raining

Silly of me I suppose to think love
Anything but a wristwatch left unwound
More accurate and it becomes only an idea
Like living outside through a Vermont winter
With birdseed and popcorn enough to last
Until the ice melts into the return of birds
Hanging buckets of song on every lawn tree
Whose hearts if it's not raining drip for real
And kids run tree to tree collecting

Some Night

While your childish heart skipped rope
Beneath a woven moon
My fingers forgot themselves
And began trusting their tiny magic

Believing the wings in your eyes
Were meant to be touched
They leapt into your sleep
Whooping to each other like cranes

You dreamt of indians on the warpath
And woke yelling for rope
With my hands on you happy as captives
Only more so

Voodoo} A Quiet Night

(for E. M. and R. P.)

You've grown tired of listening to your
    breath grate
You desire a music made without metal
Something light and airy like a diver's hair
You've named the fingers of the one you love
For the reasons you are unable to sleep
But each counting to ten changes your mind
And you are unable to name the thumbs
    correctly
Instead of 'Cruelty' and 'Bitterness'
They become 'Barbados' and 'St. Thomas'
And your fingers drum to the loud music of
    islands
The storm in your hands blows through your
    body
Whirling you into the kitchen
Where in a vase behind the dishes wait
The nail parings you were saving for a time
    like this

The Argument

When you close the door
A star falls inside each of us
Striking a line through the landscape we
    shared
Where a dreamer looking up
Sees his face reflected in a window
And says a few words into himself
About the distance he's traveled between
    dreams
Then whistling in the worn air
Closes his eyes and lifts his luggage

Permanent Weather

Looking out on the mended landscape
His hands move as though milking his worries
His wife is behind him fretting about the
    weather

But it is not this late October rain
Forcing him into silence
He is remembering his favorite barn cat
    attacking him
And disappearing from the farm forever
He hasn't told his wife that during his heart
    attack
He'd called to that cat and had seen him
The reason he'd given for stuffing his pillow
    with hay
Was that he missed the smell of the barn
Not that every night at dusk
He yearns to curl up in the hayloft alone
His sleep filled with purring

Turning to his wife he tells her
Not to worry it will change
But soon he'll be in a place with permanent
    weather

Homecoming{*An Abyss*

Someone is crying behind a door
On which you are about to knock
Filled with an azure feeling
For a prolonged moment memory whistles
Like a train crossing a bridge
You remember that old trestle
Whose shadow resembled a broad smile
And how you sat under it
Imagining yourself a tooth in your father's
    mouth
You think if only his face could do that now
And suddenly you're standing staring at
    yourself
Your face melting into your hot heart
With the sound of someone crying
The space under the door an abyss
In which all the moments of your absence
    have gathered

A Reply

Your letter was read with interest
And we look forward to your arrival
We began rehearsals last week
Not forgetting there will be
The sound of footsteps
We've added several flights of stairs
And are now hanging doors
There is considerable difficulty
Obtaining those personal noises you mentioned
But we are grateful for the diversion
The memory of your car
Slowing in the snowdrifts as it pulled away
Has taken up our interest these past months
The chains slamming and gears screaming
Combined to sound like a horse
Ripping its belly on a missed jump
Only without any sort of gallantry
We have forgiven you
Though occasionally one of us wakes
From a dream of horses
Certain that it is snowing
But what matters most is your arrival
We're anxiously waiting
For the sound of your car
To wake us with a changed voice
Now that the flowers are blooming

Onyx Windows } If It Is Night

If it is night and a voice rings
Those hearts empty as shoes
Fill with birds
If it is night and a voice rings
Those hearts empty as shoes
Fill with birds
And the flight of fear
Begins loving itself
If it is night and a voice rings
Those hearts empty as shoes
Fill with birds
And the flight of fear
Begins loving itself
Even though it is raining
Drops of light
Through the onyx windows
If it is night and a voice rings
Those hearts empty as shoes
Fill with birds
And the flight of fear
Begins loving itself
Even though it is raining
Drops of light
Through the onyx windows
And hands can be seen
Holding the albatross of morning

The First Dream

The first dream reveals death   But no one remembers the first dream   Sometimes one will claim he remembers the first dream But that is only the first dream he remembers Some religions claim to know the first dream And the dreamless believe them   But the others do not   The first dream cannot be revealed   If a person remembers the first dream that memory is death

Burning Ships

(in 1519 Cortez burned his ships at Veracruz and
led his troops into the high mountains of Mexico)

Since Cortez ordered us to burn the ships
The nights have smelled of soot
And our sleep fills with the hope of returning
    home
Even in this cold it burns our hearts
Turning them into a black smell that sticks
    in our throats
Preventing us from speaking out
    *

If where we are going appears useless
At least it will not be these mountains
Which at sunset look exactly like burning ships
    *

Every morning one or more of us has died
And some waken with tears
But if we are looked in the eyes with a
    question
We say it is the smoke from the morning fire
And look up at the sky
Where the circling birds resemble our dreams
    of sails

The Body of a Beggar

(from a conversation with Marco Jerez)

My body is the body of a beggar
Whatever is discarded by others fits me
My best shirt has a stain above the heart
Whenever I smell flowers it beats
With the sound of wedding music

All spring my shoes waltzed alone

I have tried discarding my own past
That is filled with the music of mariachis
But when I return to my room at night
It is sitting in my chair waiting for me
When I undress it embraces me
I feel its weight beside me after I am asleep
And my dreams climb the mountains of Mexico

Every morning I wake tired   smelling flowers

Hunger

This far from my country
Its language sticks to my skin
In exile I live by its echoes
I eat when the whispers
Build inside my body
Reminding me of the coast
Where my homeland
Is cut from the world
Hunger there is different
It cannot be satisfied
Even here a hollowness exists
That no amount of food can fill
Sleep comes to me as a memory
Of those nights spent traveling
Barefoot and dark
So as not to be noticed
In all my dreams my friends
Their faces blackened
Tell me I must go back
So armed with their friendship
I am returning to that hunger
Knowing it may be satisfied
Only by our deaths
And what others make of them

Innocent
Things

Richard

Jones

to my mother and father

Walking Home After Work

Coming out of the tunnel
into the cool Manhattan evening,
I feel rough hands on my heart—
women yelling over rows of vegetables
and old men cheating at cards;
cabbies cursing each other
with their fists, while the music
of church bells sails over the tenements;
and the father, angry and tired
after working all day,
embracing his little girl, kissing her
in Spanish, brushing the hair
out of her eyes so she can see.

The Mechanic

It's dark in the garage. The mechanic
goes down into the concrete grave
with his trouble light, while the day
rushes past outside on the highway.

Standing in the pit beneath an old engine,
he works patiently, with a kind of gentleness.
Looking up, he could be in a field at night
staring into the sky for answers.

In the afternoons, when the owners come
    back
for their cars, he stands around with the
    other men,
drinking beer, pushing one another around,
    cursing.
He works the kinks out of his neck, squints
    into the sun.

For My Friends

Days are spent in the meadow brooding
over lives that go on without me.
In the city, friends meet

after work in bars and talk
about music and Marx and what is wrong
with American poetry. It's summer,

still light when they go out,
walking up Columbus Avenue
to the Mexican restaurant, where

the service is slow and they can sit all night
in the courtyard, drinking beer, while
empty plates pile up around them

and night covers the square of sky
above them and lights
come on everywhere and the city is

alive, like this meadow, in summer—
a million small things buzzing with life—
as I make my way back to the farmhouse
    in the dark.

Remembering Rivers

Today I saw the river
overflowing its banks,
swimming among the trees,
which rose, silent and still,
up out of the water
like men with their eyes closed.

I saw this from my car,
stopped on a low bridge.
As I looked at the water
I remembered rivers I'd seen as a child,
remembered waiting for storms to pass,
the river crawling toward the house,
and afterwards scavenging the debris
of fallen trees, dead things, earth.

Remembering how it felt
to stand and stare at rivers,
I wanted to believe that child still lived,
standing at the edge.
Instead, as I sped away,
turning the car up the hill,
I felt only like a man running away,
the dark water rising below.

The Dinner Party

In the candlelight, we are eating and laughing and talking about the future, about the children we all hope to have. One man says this is a moral question, saying he is not sure he wants to be the father of a child who must live in this world.

"If I want to have a child, I will," one woman says, turning to my wife to tell of the things she will give her child, everything she wanted but couldn't have.

My child will also have things other children do not have—nights like these, warm evenings, the winter far away outside, until a window is opened for air.

The laughter of strangers below in the street couples with the candles' sputter, and for the first time tonight we fall silent, the thorns of light in our faces going out all at once.

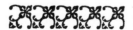

Writing Poetry on Black Paper

You get up, try the phone,
but the wires have been cut.

Suddenly there is a pounding
on the door. You imagine
women in torn gowns. It is
Paganini. He smashes
your ex-girlfriend's violin,
waves his white scarf,
and dashes into the woods.

You walk outside, sit on the stoop.
All night
the stars drop
like white coins
into the black cup of the meadow.

Pastoral

October afternoon. The hunters
shooting the sky
will soon turn and march
across the half-harvested fields

to count the kill over drinks.
Everyone agrees the day is fine,
laughs when a child runs away
with a dead dove, making it fly.

Distant guns; the evening sky is red.
When will it end, those explosions
inside you, the doves who live
inside the heart, being shot, one by one?

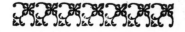

The Public Garden

She closes the gate
of the public garden
behind her, an autumn garden
enclosed by walls, no flowers
only bare fruit trees
and the intimation
of bad weather.
I'm by myself on the bench,
the leaves, like the children
we talk about having,
racing back and forth
in the windy sunshine
at my feet. It's a scene
we know by heart—
the careful voices,
the careful good-byes.
We've learned it is better
not to talk at times like this
but to leave quietly when
we must, the only sound
the click of a lock.
The afternoon caught
between apple trees
twisted in thought
and pomegranates blooming
along the north wall,

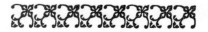

I count the bricks, the money
we'll need next week,
the children we don't have.
This small garden
is the perfect place
for my angry heart,
the perfect space,
a small square of life
that is walled in, like me,
waiting for her to come back,
to come back inside.

After the Quarrel

The sky and I are wide awake.
I go out and prowl around the house in the
  dark
to get an idea of what I'll look like when
  I'm asleep.
In a high window, the fan is turning quietly,
  like a propeller.
She is already there, drifting along, her sleep
  carrying her like a ship.

*

The earth and I wander around in circles.
I stand under the walnut tree and open my
  arms wide.
Rain comes, but with none of the answers
  I need.
I think I'm alone, but then
something moves behind me—
the moon, appearing and disappearing
  behind the clouds.

*

It rained last night, and the morning is cool
and damp, as if all the leaves had fallen. She
pulls her blue robe tight around her, pours
coffee. Her eyes have that black intensity of
flashbulbs, a second after the picture has been
taken. I stand before her, surrounded by
light.

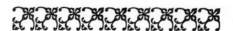

The Flower Box

A man builds a small wooden box
the size, let's say, of his wife's hand,
something he can fill with flowers
which, as they dry and turn brown,
give up their moisture and fragrance
to the wood, which will hold it
like love, in its hand, forever.

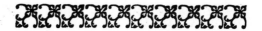

Innocent Things

Sometimes I need to look
only for innocent things—
the trees lined up along the ridge,
or the geese I hear before seeing them
floating over the treetops in a V,
as if it were the sign for peace,
for victory over a divided world.

Or maybe there are no innocent things,
only the sound their wings make
when the leader ceases to call out
and, all at once, wings turn down,
and there is the sound of wind,
of angels coming down to bless us.

FISSION

Barry Sternlieb

To my mother
and in memory of my father

Oracle

for Maureen

She's in the garden
working the warp
of rows while I stare
at how union

grows lush and nourishing,
each spring turning hope
into ground with eyes
for this alone,

and as need now reflects
the harvest: ingress,
egress, gathering time
in old bushel baskets,

solitude is her love
for land, for the plants
she embodies
gone slowly to seed.

Fission

*U*ntil now it's been No
when my daughters have asked
to explore this graveyard
on Route 41, but today
is cold for late September
and sky bares that clarity
dreams never touch.
Raising the shades at dawn
I saw a wasp lose hold
of an eave
and drop into grass, the black
plumbline of gravity
soluble in light,
and me, staring through the window,
drawn slowly toward stillness
that breathes here
as I make these stones live,
reading each inscription
down a polished row.

While we walk, I offer
my poor sense of beauty,
saying none are born
without the dark tapping
lightly on their eyes,
but it's my usual blind
search for words and I think

better keep to the facts:
the granite names,
the bones, the worms.
Nothing I can say
will mean more
than one grave,
remembering my own
first look, how the stone cell
held genes for infinity
tight enough to break.

As questions rain
I leave the path
to sit beside a huge elm
whose dying confession
is a halfmoon of fungus
and a few bare branches
reminding me that the simplest
life will age
to the verge of death
then blindly divide
into daughters.

Homecoming

*B*ecause it was time to forgive,
one by one, our children came home.

First the eldest, the she-wolf,
light fur bristling,
loped toward the rise of her name.

Then, around noon, a son appeared
in the crown of the dead elm: a flame-
eyed hawk, tempered by distance.

Over the years, the past
had often changed hands
until we learned to expect nothing,
yet slowly, this day,
they found their way back.

Windwise, the shy girl, the lynx,
ears erect, stalked unblinking
at her purpose, and a river
tore north in our hearts.

Now, with their return,
we dared not reach out or speak,
but instead kept still as a loss
of memory or desire, alone together,

mated for life, while our youngest,
the green snake,
moved sleeplike through the sun
and onto the porch, purest grace
we had missed much too long.

Then came the moon-souled buck,
and snow goose, and immersed in strength,
the great glistening black bear.

By dusk, as horizon approached
the color of depth, all had come back
to their birthplace,
where blood could assume a family,

back to bodies before claws
and fur, scales and wings,

to lives we had once conceived
in the way before the war.

For the Farm Ghost

*Y*our barn needs work.
The warped boards are diaries of rain,
quietly incoherent,
and more than ever, neglect speaks
for distance, letting termites comb
years out of wood.
All day long, in a living gesture,
it seems to lean slowly toward evening.

Our eyes become lost on the inroads
of the place
as luminous dust veers into breath
and walls read like love
for loss, for the green
of essentials mulched by age.

Around here, as the saying goes, a soul
will follow the grain
and though a century's gone
a caul of silence clings
when I allude to you
in the shattered panes and split beams,
in the foothold of sky
on a dangerous roof.

Provision

*I*t's become a question of fear,
the ceremonial winterizing. This year

I found the pumphouse roof gnawed
bare in three patches by the wood-

chuck who is either immortal
or bulletproof, and the A-frame tooled

by carpenter ants. Now,
in fall, with a dawn coup

of frost changing everything, I gut
the small house, yank the rat-

mazed insulation out and crowbar
the riddled wood. It's more dark

than light and the suspense of being
alone here in silence is enough to ring

the east like a vast spectral bell,
one violet note holding all.

For Kyla, Age 3

*T*onight I read my daughter
the story of a Cree hunter

who has killed his first birds
in early spring, the Moon of Geese.

He prepares and cooks them himself,
keeping his family silent

during the meal or the bird spirits,
which are stronger than the birds,

might grow angry and change the season's
luck from good to bad.

When all have finished eating,
he collects the bones and sings them

into the fire where they are purified
and returned by way of ashes

to the heart of things: earth and water.
My daughter takes the book

she is too young to read, the wings
of its pages alive in her hands,

and wants to know what happens next.
Already, the hunger begins.

Gardener

*W*ith gin wisdom
and borrowed gun, tonight
he'll kill the thief.

The west turns bronze
on his arms
and mosquitoes float from the birch.

He can hear a blurred voice now.
It rings along a neglected route
of his mind

and he follows until the song
becomes a nymph
beckoning him bed down,
but in the delicate lull

between the woman
that is thought
and the one that is touched,

a woodchuck
finds the damp
budding plants it loves.

Origami

*F*or the last time
hold our children close.
First the older, who will slowly
forget you, and then the baby
who touches your delicate mouth,
each smooth eyefold, and that fragrant
sleep-colored hair.

You must have felt the journey
come to life before we understood
what was happening, an October-like
change in countenance, a pond
abandoned.

But the peaks of your voice
are crystalline with new growth,
acceptance channeling sun into pulse
as our daughters give way
just enough to watch your hands spawn
a swan from paper, deftly,
arced neck and impossible
wings appear.

Inside minutes, complete,
it's set on the mantel
between bronze stag and earthen ram;
suddenly faced

with your leaving,
we cannot fathom the intricacy
of so controlled a flight, your mind
performing as if nourished by loss
for a thousand fragile years.

Balance of Power

*I*t does me good
to watch cold come to light
in these hills
because I'm through
splitting a winter
of birch and maple,
and pipe lit, collar up,
feel the burning
heart in horizon
stop long enough to recall
tomorrow you will be gone
ten years. Geese will wave
past the house, and old hornets,
drunk on sun, will stagger
from clothesline to porchrail.
The urge to fly has brought me
the happiness of knowing
I can't. Look down that road:
Wind relays the quiet
belief in life
lasting another day.

Appendix I.

The Chapbooks: A Bibliography

THE NECESSITIES, Gary Metras

15 pages. 5½ x 8½ inches. Edition of 200 copies. Display type is 24 and 36 point Garamond Old Style. Text set in 10 pt. Century Schoolbook on 4 pt. leading. (Type for this anthology was reset in 12 pt. Garamond O.S. on 4 pt. leading.) Black ink used throughout. Paper is Strathmore Artlaid II Green text and Grandee Barcelona Gray for wrap around cover. Some copies also used Green Linenweave and/or light blue Circa Laid for endwrappers. Cover illustration is a metal etching of an extinct fern. Single handsewn signature. Publication date: December 1979. Out of print.

CITY PAUSES, Andy Gunderson

18 pages. 5 x 8 inches. Edition of 200 copies. Display type is 24 pt. Frascati. Text set in 10 pt. Goudy Old Style Bold on 2 pt. leading. Cover title is linoleum block cut. Black ink used for text throughout. Two color cover and title page: red and black. Paper is Strathmore Grandee Mantilla Ivory text and Americana Alamo Tan for wrap around cover. Single handsewn signature. Publication date: May 1980. Out of print.

FROM AN AGE OF CARS, Merritt Clifton

23 pages. 5½ x 8 inches. Editon of 200 copies, 10 of which were printed two colors throughout (red titles and black text). Display type is 14 and 24 pt. Highspot. Text set in 10 pt. News Gothic on 2 pt. leading, with one poem, "Verdict," set on 4 pt. leading. Cover illustration is lino block cut. Black ink used throughout regular editon. Two color cover: red and black. Paper is Strathmore Grandee

Mantilla Ivory text and Americana Prairie Gold cover. Single handsewn signature. Publication date: August 1980.

MATTERS OF THE HEART, W. D. Ehrhart

23 pages. 5 x 8 inches. Edition of 325 copies. Display type is 24 pt. Frascati and Highspot, with Frascati also used for initial letters of text. Cover title is lino block cut. Text set in 10 pt. Goudy O.S. Bold on 4 pt. leading. Black ink used throughout for text with the title page having red rules setting off the black title; cover printed in dark blue. Paper is Strathmore Artlaid II Natural text and Americana Salem Red cover. Single handsewn signature. Publication date: May 1981. Out of print.

DON'T DRESS YOUR CAT IN AN APRON,
Laurel Speer

18 pages. 5¼ x 8½ inches. Edition of 300 copies. Display type is 24 pt. Highspot on cover, title page and initial letters of text. Poem titles set in 10 pt. Century Roman Italic. Text set in 10 pt. Goudy O.S. Bold on 4 pt. leading. Cover title is lino block cut. Black ink used throughout for text. Cover printed in brown ink. Title page printed black with red border piece decorations. Paper is Hammermill Vellum White text with Strathmore Grandee Spanish Gold cover and Grandee Cordoba Brown endwrapper. Single handsewn signature. Publication date: August 1981. Out of print.

WINDOWS AND WALLS, Richard Jones

20 pages. 5¼ x 8½ inches. Editon of 200 copies. Display type is 18 and 24 pt. Cochin Open. Text set in 12 pt. Garamond O.S. on 2 pt. leading. Metal cut spider used for decoration at foot of text pages.

Black ink used throughout. Three color cover and title pages: black letters with a red brick-like border and dark blue rule. Paper is Mohawk Artemis Ivory text, Strathmore Grandee Pyranees White cover and Grandee Navarre Blue endwrapper. Single hand-sewn signature. Publication date: August 1982. Out of print.

PETALS FROM THE WOMANFLOWER,
Margaret Key Biggs

18 pages. $5\frac{1}{4}$ x $8\frac{1}{2}$ inches. Edition of 300 copies. Display type is 24 pt. Century Old Style Italic. Poem titles set in 12 pt. Garamond O.S. Text set in 12 pt. Garamond O.S. Italic on 4 pt. leading. 12 pt. border pieces used for decoration on cover and head and foot of text pages. Black ink used throughout. Two color cover: red and black. Paper is Mohawk Ticonderoga Ivory text, Strathmore Brigadoon Paisley Yellow cover and Brigadoon Ancient Red endwrapper. Single handsewn signature. Publication date: January 1983.

PHILIPPE AT HIS BATH, Constance Pierce

26 pages. 6 x 9 inches. Edition of 270 copies with 25 copies signed & numbered by the author. Display type is 24 pt. Century O.S. Italic. Enlarged cover initial is lino block cut. Text set in 12 pt. Garamond O.S. on 2 pt. leading with 24 pt. Swash Initials at stanza beginnings. Etched copper cut used for frontispiece. Swash decorations on title page and foot of text pages. Black ink used throughout. Two color cover and title pages: medium blue and dark blue for cover and medium blue and black for title page. Paper is Mohawk Artemis Radiant White deckle text with Tan cover. Single handsewn signature. Publication date: November 1983.

ROBBING THE PILLARS, Harry Humes

27 pages. $5\frac{1}{4}$ x $8\frac{1}{4}$ inches. Edition of 300 copies with 25 copies signed & numbered by the author. Display type is 14 and 18 pt. Century Old Style Bold. Text set in 12 pt. Garamond O.S. on 2 pt. leading. Lino block cut designs on cover and four interior pages; open and solid squares as additional decorations at the head and foot of text pages. Black ink used throughout. Two color cover and title pages: medium blue and black. Paper is Circa Laid Gray text with Mohawk Artemis Gray cover. Single handsewn signature. Publication date: March 1984.

MENTIONING DREAMS, Michael Rattee

30 pages. $5\frac{1}{2}$ x $8\frac{1}{2}$ inches. Edition of 250 copies. Display type is 24 and 36 pt. Garamond O.S. on cover and title pages with 14 pt. Garamond Italic Bold poem titles. Text set in 12 pt. Garamond O.S. on 2 pt. leading with 24 pt. Frascati initial letters. Black ink used throughout. Two color title page: black letters with medium blue metal cut decorations. Three color cover: green, gold and red; cover decoration made with 24 pt. metal cut birds arranged in an oval of three colors with the sixth row blind stamped. Paper is Strathmore Grandee Lugo Gray text and Navarre Blue cover. Sewn with whip stitch. Publication date: September 1985.

INNOCENT THINGS, Richard Jones

16 unnumbered pages. $5\frac{1}{2}$ x $8\frac{1}{2}$ inches. Edition of 220 copies. Display type is 24 and 36 pt. Garamond O.S. on cover and title pages with 14 pt. Garamond Bold poem titles. Text set in 12 pt. Garamond O.S. with Monotype initials. 24 pt. Monotype border pieces are used for cover decoration and at the foot of text pages. Black ink throughout. Two color cover

and title pages: brown letters and red decorations with the cover having an additional border blind stamped. Paper is Strathmore Grandee Lugo Gray text, Basque Brown endwrapper, Mantilla Ivory cover and Hammermill Vellum cover Apache Red endpapers. Single handsewn signature. Publication date: December 1985.

FISSION, Barry Sternlieb

16 unnumbered pages. $5\frac{1}{2}$ x $8\frac{1}{2}$ inches. Edition of 165 numbered copies. Display type is 48 pt. Roman, 24 and 36 pt. Garamond O.S. with poem titles set in 14 pt. Garamond Bold. Text set in 12 pt. Garamond O.S. on 2 pt. leading with 24 pt. Swash initial letters. Dragonfly metal cut decoration used at foot of text pages with metal cut leaf on title page and cover. Black ink used throughout. Two color cover and title pages: black letters and green leaves. Paper is Strathmore Grandee Pyranees White text, Lugo Gray cover with Hammermill Opaque Lime Green endwrapper and Hammermill Vellum cover Spring Green endpapers. Single handsewn signature. The author assisted in all phases of production. Publication date: September 1986.

Appendix II.

Author Notes

Margaret Key Biggs

is the author of four other poetry collections: THE PLUMAGE OF THE SUN (Negative Capability Press), SWAMPFIRE (Samisdat), SISTER TO THE SUN (Earthwise) and MAGNOLIAS AND SUCH (Red Key Press). Biggs recently left high school teaching to write fulltime and conduct writing workshops. Born in Alabama, Biggs lives in Florida.

Merritt Clifton

is the editor & publisher of Samisdat since 1973. Clifton also describes himself as a freelance newspaper hack, a baseball historian and a semi-pro marathon runner. In 1980 he was honored for pioneering expose on acid rain by the Society for Investigative Journalism and in 1984 for distinguished work on water quality by Environment Quebec. Clifton is the author of numerous books and chapbooks: fiction, poetry, history, bibliography, expose and how-to. He grew up in what he calls Berzerkeley, California and has been a resident of Brigham, Quebec since 1977. Clifton is married to author, artist & farmer June Kemp.

W.D. Ehrhart

writes and teaches in Philadelphia, Pennsylvania where he also lives with his wife, Anne. His poetry books include THE SAMISDAT POEMS (Samisdat Press), TO THOSE WHO HAVE GONE HOME TIRED (Thunder's Mouth Press) and THE OUTER BANKS (Adastra); he is the author of the prose books: VIETNAM-PERKASIE (McFarland; Zebra reprint) and MARKING TIME (Avon); he is the editor of CARRYING THE DARKNESS (Avon) and contributing editor to THOSE WHO WERE THERE (Dustbooks).

Andy Gunderson

is a self-educated writer with a love for nature and simplicity, as his contribution to this anthology, which was written about and mostly in the city parks of Minneapolis, show. He's worked at various jobs from cab driving to cooking, janitorial to factory work. For a couple of years he published & edited the literary journal UNDERGROUND RAG MAG. He lives in Rochester, Minnesota.

Richard Jones

was born in London in 1953. He was educated at the University of Virginia, and has taught at Ripon College, Vermont College and the University of Virginia. In addition to his two chapbooks from Adastra, he is the author of COUNTRY OF AIR (Copper Canyon Press) and WALK ON (Alderman Press). He has edited two critical anthologies, POETRY AND POLITICS (William Morrow & Co.) and OF SOLITUDE AND SILENCE: WRITINGS ON ROBERT BLY (Beacon Press). He is the editor of the literary journal, Poetry East, for which he won a CCLM Editor's Award for 1985.

Harry Humes'

first book of poems, WINTER WEEDS, was the Devins Award for poetry winner in 1983 and was published in that year by the University of Missouri Press. His second book of poetry, GATHERING WATERCRESS IN THE HEX COUNTRY, was published in late 1986 by Owl Creek Press. He is currently the recipient of a Pennsylvania Council of the Arts Literary Fellowship. Additionally, he edits the poetry journal, Yarrow. His poems have appeared in such journals as The Virginia Quarterly Review, Poetry Northwest, Shenandoah, Salmagundi, The Massachusetts Review, and CutBank. He lives in the country in Pennsylvania with his wife and new daughter, and fishes for trout with dry flies as often as he can.

Gary Metras

born 1947 in Holyoke, Massa-
chusetts and raised in nearby
Chicopee;   currently   lives
in Easthampton, Mass. with
his wife, Natalie, and two
children, Jason and Nadia.
He holds degrees from the
University of Massachusetts
at Amherst and Goddard
College. He teaches high
school English. His poetry
books include CENTER
OF THE SPIRAL (Timberline
Press), DESTINY'S CALEN-
DAR (Samisdat) and THE
NIGHT WATCHES (Adastra).
He is the editor & publisher
of Adastra Press.

Constance Pierce

born 1943 in Virginia. Grew
up in Virginia, North Caro-
lina and Germany. Associate
Professor in English Depart-
ment at Miami (Ohio) Uni-
versity. Taught at universi-
ties in Puerto Rico and
Portugal. Recieved fellow-
ships from the National
Endowment for the Arts
and the National Endowment
for the Humanities. A
book of short stories, WHEN
THINGS GET BACK TO
NORMAL (Illinois State
University and the Fiction
Collective) published in 1986. Also writes criticism
on literature and film.

Michael Rattee

born 1953 in Holyoke, Mass., grew up in Randolph, Vermont, he now makes his home in Tucson, Arizona with his wife, Hannelore. After various factory and maintenance jobs, he is currently self-employed as a design painter and occasionally guest lectures on poetry. He and Hannelore have organized reading series in Tucson. He is editor of the poetry magazine, Prickly Pear/Tucson. In 1984 he was awarded a Fellowship from the National Endowment for the Arts. He is also author of CALLING YOURSELF HOME (Cleveland State University Press).

Laurel Speer

has published a dozen books; her two latest poetry collections are VINCENT ET AL and THE SCANDAL OF HER BATH. Her poems have appeared in numerous journals including, most recently, New York Quarterly, New Letters, Kansas Quarterly and Mid-American Review. She makes her home in Tucson.

Barry Sternlieb

 born 1947 in New York City. Educated at Fairleigh Dickinson University. Taught elementary school in the Bronx for five years and then moved to the Berkshires. Presently lives in Richmond, Mass. with his wife, Maureen, and their two daughters, Kirsten & Kyla. He teaches in nearby Pittsfield. His work has appeared in various journals including Longhouse, Poetry, Prairie Schooner, Samisdat and The Minnesota Review. FISSION is his first collection.

Appendix III.

Checklist of Complete Publications

NOTE: width precedes height in dimensions. Titles marked OP are Out of Print. All editions, except reprints, are handcrafted: hand set type, hand fed letterpress printed, hand sewn signatures. Books with fewer than 48 pages have a single signature while longer books have two signatures. Covers are square spine paper wrappers. Cloth covers, where indicated, are also handcrafted. Design and production, except offset reprints, is by Gary Metras. Titles marked * are reprinted in THE ADASTRA READER.

The Necessities*
By Gary Metras. 15pp. 5½ x 8½ inches. 200 copies. ISBN 0-938566-01-6. OP.   1979

City Pauses *
By Andy Gunderson. 18pp. 5x8. 200 copies. ISBN 0-938566-02-4. OP.   1980

From an Age of Cars *
By Merritt Clifton. 23pp. 5½x8. 200 copies. ISBN 0-938566-03-2.   1980

Nuclear Quartet
Folded broadsheet. 16 x 8½. 450 copies. One anti-nuke poem each by Merritt Clifton, Mirian Sagan, W.D.Ehrhart, Gary Metras.OP. 1980

Matters of the Heart*
By W.D. Ehrhart. 23pp. 5 x 8. 325 copies. ISBN 0-938566-04-0. OP.   1981

Don't Dress Your Cat in an Apron *
By Laurel Speer. 18pp. 5¼ x 8½. 300copies. ISBN 0-938566-05-9. OP.   1981

The Night Watches
By Gary Metras. 48pp. 5½ x 8½. 400 copies. ISBN 0-938566-06-7 paper wrappers. ISBN 0-938566-07-5 cloth. ISBN 0-938566-08-1 cloth, signed&numbered. 1981

Pleasure Boat
Poems and block cuts by Nyuka. 24pp.$5\frac{1}{2}$x$8\frac{1}{2}$.
60 signed & numbered copies. Printed for
the author and carried in the Adastra
catalogue. ISBN 0-938566-09-1. OP.   **1981**

Struggle for the Dawn
By Norman R. Bissell. 20pp. $5\frac{1}{2}$ x 8. 220
copies. Printed for the author and carried
in the Adastra catalogue.
ISBN 0-938566-10-5. OP.   **1982**

Windows and Walls *
By Richard Jones. 20pp. $5\frac{1}{4}$x$8\frac{1}{2}$. 200 copies.
ISBN 0-938566-11-3. OP.   **1982**

Something More Than Force: Poems for
Guatemala, 1971-1982
By Zoe Anglesey. 48pp. $5\frac{1}{2}$ x $8\frac{1}{4}$. 300copies.
ISBN 0-938566-12-1 paper wrapper.
ISBN 0-938566-13-X cloth signed&no'd 1-25. **1982**
Reprinted photo-offset. ISBN 0-938566-21-0. **1984**

Petals from the Womanflower *
By Margaret Key Biggs. 18pp. $5\frac{1}{4}$ x $8\frac{1}{2}$. 300
copies. ISBN 0-938566-14-8.   **1983**

No Dreams for Sale
By D. Roger Martin. 56pp. $5\frac{1}{2}$ x $8\frac{1}{4}$. 300
copies. ISBN 0-938566-15-6 paper wrapper.
ISBN 0-938566-16-4 cloth signed&no'd 1-25. **1983**

Philippe at His Bath*
By Constance Pierce. 26pp. 6x9. 270copies.
ISBN 0-938566-17-2
ISBN 0-938566-18-0 signed & no'd 1-25.   **1983**

Robbing the Pillars*
By Harry Humes. 27pp. $5\frac{1}{4}$ x $8\frac{1}{4}$. 300 copies.
ISBN 0-938566-19-9
ISBN 0-938566-20-2 signed & no'd 1-25.   **1984**

The Outer Banks & Other Poems
By W.D. Ehrhart. 52pp. 5¼ x 8¼. 300copies.
ISBN 0-938566-22-9 paper wrapper. OP.
ISBN 0-938566-23-7 cloth signed & numbered
1-25. OP.   1984
Reprinted photo-offset, perfect bound.
ISBN 0-938566-28-8.   1985

Other Lives
By Peter Oresick. 48pp. 5½x8¼. 275 copies.
ISBN 0-938566-24-5 paper wrapper. OP.
ISBN 0-938566-25-3 cloth signed &no'd. OP. 1985
Reprinted photo-offset, perfect bound.
ISBN 0-938566-29-6.   1985

Mentioning Dreams*
By Michael Rattee. 30pp. 5½x8½. 250copies.
ISBN 0-938566-26-1.   1985

Innocent Things*
By Richard Jones. 11 poems unpaged. 5½x8½.
220 copies. ISBN 0-938566-30-X.   1985

Fission*
By Barry Sternlieb. 9poems unpaged. 5½x8½.
165 numbered copies. ISBN 0-938566-31-8.   1986
OP.

INDEX of Poem Titles